"In her new book, Celia Hodent offers a brilliant journey into the psychology of videogames. This book provides not only an insightful analysis of the psychological processes engaged in all types of games but also how to nurture such processes to make videogames fun and meaningful for the players. Importantly, Celia Hodent doesn't shy away from the difficult questions: she discusses thoroughly, in an honest and scientific way, the potential benefits and negative effects of videogames and the ethical issues raised by using psychology to create videogames. A definite must-have for all the gaming community but also for everyone interested in the growing role that psychology and psychologists play in UX."

—**Grégoire Borst**, Professor of Developmental Psychology,
Université de Paris, and Director of LaPsyDÉ
(CNRS), France

"*The Psychology of Video Games* is a must-read for anyone who wants to understand the vast and pixelated minefield of video game research. It not only gets under the psychological hood of why we play games, but also how these games impact both players and society. Readers will quickly discover that, like the tiny, round classic video game character Kirby, *The Psychology of Video Games* is filled with way more information than seems possible given its concise size."

—**Patrick M. Markey**, Professor of Psychology at
Villanova University and coauthor of *Moral Combat:
Why the War on Violent Video Games Is Wrong*

"It's been said that good video games are engaging because they are actually psychology at play. Nowhere is that more evident than in Celia Hodent's latest book, *The Psychology of Video Games*. Thought-provoking and fascinating, her book provides a practical and empirical case for why we find video games so enjoyable to play. If you want to know more about the intersectionality of cognitive neuroscience and user-centered design, look no further!"

—**Matthew Farber**, EdD, Assistant Professor at University of
Northern Colorado and author of *Gamify Your Classroom* and
Game-Based Learning in Action

THE PSYCHOLOGY
OF VIDEO GAMES

What impact can video games have on players? How does psychology influence video game creation? Why do some games become cultural phenomena?

The Psychology of Video Games explores the relationship between psychology and video games from the perspective of both game developers and players. It looks at how games are made and what makes them fun and successful, the benefits gaming can have on players in relation to education and health care, concerns over potential negative impacts such as pathological gaming, and ethics considerations.

With gaming being one of the most popular forms of entertainment today, *The Psychology of Video Games* shows the important role played by an understanding of the human brain and its mental processes in the development of ethical and inclusive video games.

Celia Hodent is a PhD in psychology and an independent consultant, providing guidance on the topics of game user experience (UX), ethics, and inclusion. She has over 10 years' experience working with game studios, including Ubisoft, LucasArts, and Epic Games (*Fortnite*).

THE PSYCHOLOGY OF EVERYTHING

People are fascinated by psychology, and what makes humans tick. Why do we think and behave the way we do? We've all met armchair psychologists claiming to have the answers, and people that ask if psychologists can tell what they're thinking. The Psychology of Everything is a series of books which debunk the popular myths and pseudo-science surrounding some of life's biggest questions.

The series explores the hidden psychological factors that drive us, from our subconscious desires and aversions, to our natural social instincts. Absorbing, informative, and always intriguing, each book is written by an expert in the field, examining how research-based knowledge compares with popular wisdom, and showing how psychology can truly enrich our understanding of modern life.

Applying a psychological lens to an array of topics and contemporary concerns – from sex, to fashion, to conspiracy theories – The Psychology of Everything will make you look at everything in a new way.

Titles in the series:

For further information about this series please visit
www.routledgetextbooks.com/textbooks/thepsychologyofeverything/

THE PSYCHOLOGY OF VIDEO GAMES

CELIA HODENT

Routledge
Taylor & Francis Group

LONDON AND NEW YORK

First published 2021
by Routledge
2 Park Square, Milton Park, Abingdon, Oxon OX14 4RN

and by Routledge
52 Vanderbilt Avenue, New York, NY 10017

Routledge is an imprint of the Taylor & Francis Group, an informa business

British Library Cataloguing-in-Publication Data
A catalogue record for this book is available from the British Library

Library of Congress Cataloging-in-Publication Data
A catalog record has been requested for this book

ISBN: 978-0-367-49312-7 (hbk)
ISBN: 978-0-367-49313-4 (pbk)
ISBN: 978-1-003-04567-0 (ebk)

Typeset in Joanna
by Apex CoVantage, LLC

CONTENTS

ACKNOWLEDGEMENTS

It was important for me to offer an approachable perspective regarding the psychology of video games that was also as precise as possible, and I hope that I've reached my goal. But I could not have done it without help. I would like to warmly thank all the people who proofread this book, offered me new perspectives, and debated the studies mentioned in this book. In particular, I would like to thank Fran Blumberg, who is always here when I need her; Chad Lane; Séverine Erhel; Darren Sugg; and Chris Ferguson. I would also like to thank Eleanor Taylor for offering me this opportunity and for her patience all throughout this adventure, especially towards the end as the coronavirus pandemic raged and greatly disturbed our ability to concentrate, to say the least. I can always count on the support of my close friends and family, so I'm addressing them my gratitude as well. Lastly, I would like to thank all the people who have been interested in chatting with me about UX, psychology, and video games, and I would like to thank all of you who are reading these lines!

INTRODUCTION

WHAT MAKES CERTAIN GAMES FUN?

Do you regularly play games, such as card games, board games, sports games, video games, or other games? If you don't, can you remember the games you used to play as a child? Some of those games didn't really catch your attention. Others you engaged in regularly, alone or with friends and family. Maybe there are some games that you've been playing and enjoying all your life, such as chess, poker, soccer (or football), Tetris, or Pokémon. If you love playing games, you know they aren't all equally engaging and fun, and that's also the case with video games. However, video games are one of the most popular forms of entertainment today and are generating a lot of interest. For example, Microsoft revealed to Business Insider in September 2019 that the game Minecraft, very popular among children, had a whopping 112 million players every month.[1] Video games are celebrated for their gameplay diversity, as they let you be the hero of an epic adventure (e.g. Uncharted series), build your own spacecraft (e.g. Kerbal Space Program), solve puzzles by manipulating space (e.g. Portal) or time (e.g. Braid), explore schizophrenia (e.g. Hellblade: Senua's Sacrifice) or depression (e.g. Sea of Solitude), and much more. The possibilities they offer are endless, and some people consider video games to be a powerful tool for education and health, and to overall make the world a better place (McGonigal, 2011).

What is it exactly that makes certain video games so compelling? Of course, your own personal taste is a factor to consider: even highly popular games aren't engaging everyone, and some niche games are highly appreciated by some dedicated players. But aside from individual preferences, some ingredients exist that can help game developers craft more engaging games, and psychology has an important role to play in helping developers identify these ingredients and then find and nurture the right recipe during the development process. Making games is hard, and many projects fail. A lot of attention is given to highly successful games that are making a lot of money, but in reality, many game studios and independent game developers are struggling to make a living. Even established studios that developed games using a popular intellectual property, such as The Walking Dead (Telltale Games), can abruptly shut down, laying off hundreds of workers, sometimes leaving them without severance pay or health insurance from one day to the next.[2] People enjoying games often don't have any idea how they are made. It's not an easy endeavor, the pressure can be high, and the working conditions are not necessarily playful, as overtime is quite common in the game industry. Many projects miss the mark and end up not being fun or sufficiently successful to survive among the thousands of games released every year, many of which being free (free to play).

When you experience a game (or anything else), it all happens in your mind. Understanding the rules, learning how to master the game, cooperating or competing with other players, overcoming challenges, feeling the thrill of winning, or dealing with the frustration of losing – it all happens in the brain. This is why understanding mental processes overall is a great starting point to grasp what makes a good game. The first two chapters of this book are dedicated to the **psychology behind making games**. Chapter 1 gives a quick overview of how the brain processes information – including when we play a video game – and its main limitations. We tackle perception, memory, attention, motivation, and emotion. This should provide the base knowledge needed before we can talk about "game user experience" in Chapter 2. User experience (UX) is a mindset allowing product developers to always keep their target audience at the center of the development process. It's about anticipating all the friction points that users might experience as they use a product, testing the product in development to verify that the developers are on the right track and, if not, how to fix it. Applied to video games, the UX mindset is about not only ensuring players won't have any difficulty interacting with the game and understanding how it works but also that the game will be fun and engaging. When all the stars align, a usable and engaging game is released, and its audience can then enjoy it.

WHAT IS THE IMPACT OF PLAYING VIDEO GAMES?

Video games are everywhere, and they are extremely popular. This raises the question of what impact they might have on players. Video games are sometimes praised for their educational and overall well-being value, and they are sometimes accused of "hooking" players, or even influencing them to commit violent acts. We will take a look at these claims in Chapters 3 and 4, which are dedicated to the **psychology of playing games**. Chapter 3 focuses on the potential benefits of playing games. We will highlight the evidence-based benefits of playing games while toning down some exaggerated enthusiasm, especially regarding "educational games". Chapter 4 focuses on the potential negative aspects of video games and on all the controversies among scholars regarding these claims. Lastly, Chapter 5 explores the ethical considerations that this popular interactive art form is raising so that video games can continue to offer engaging experiences while being respectful of all players.

I hope that you will enjoy your reading!

1

OUR BRAINS ON VIDEO GAMES

Whatever you do in life, whether it is playing a video game, watching a movie, listening to a conversation, working, or reading this book, the experience happens in your mind. The term "mind" refers to our mental processes, such as attention and memory, which are a product of the brain (and the body). Therefore, we first need to consider how the brain works to understand the psychology of what makes games fun. There are some subtle differences between the mind and the brain, but since that is not the topic of this book, I will simplify and use the terms "brain" and "mind" interchangeably here. Remember, though, that the brain is extremely complex and it remains a mystery for the most part. What I will describe here is a simplification of our current limited understanding of the human brain. The scientific study of the mind is called "cognitive science", and it includes multiple disciplines such as psychology, neuroscience, and computer science. Thanks to research in cognitive science, we have an overall understanding of how the brain processes information and learns, which is represented in a very simplified chart in Figure 1.1.

In reality, we do not have independent compartments dedicated to specific mental functions, but this chart allows us to approximately grasp what's going on in our brain when we process information. This "process" usually starts with the perception of stimuli (inputs) from our environment that are conveyed by our many senses, and it ends with modifications in our memory via synaptic modifications in the

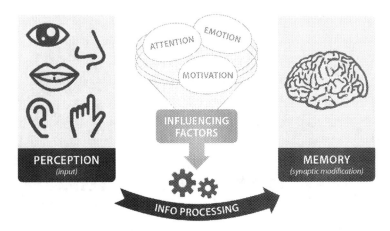

Figure 1.1 A very simplified chart of how the brain learns and processes information (from Hodent, 2017)

brain – for example, new synapses (the connections between neurons) can be established. Yes, it means that playing video games is "rewiring" your brain but so is anything you do in life, even reading these lines. And that's because the brain is not hardwired in the first place; it's malleable and will adjust depending on our perception and interaction with our ever-changing environment. This "brain plasticity" is what allows us to adapt and survive. From perception to memory, a complex process is taking place and is influenced by many factors. First and foremost, our level of attention has a considerable impact on the quality of information processing and therefore the quality of learning. For instance, if it's difficult for you to pay attention to what a speaker is saying at a conference because a coworker is pinging you about some urgent matter, you won't learn about the content covered by the speaker as efficiently as you would if you were giving the speaker your full and undivided attention. Attention is, in turn, affected by our motivation and our emotion. Other factors are impacting information processing, but we will focus on the ones aforementioned.

I will briefly describe perception, memory, attention, motivation, and emotion to give you an overview of how the brain processes information and, more specifically, what are its main limitations. Even though I'm describing each element separately and in a certain order, they are not separate entities working independently one after the other. In fact, the brain does not even "process" information like a computer would because the brain is not a computer. We use a lot of terms originating from computers simply because they are familiar and help us comprehend how the brain works. In reality, the brain is a living organ that is too complex for us to understand precisely. Ironically enough, our brains are also too limited to fully understand its complexity . . . but let's not fall into this rabbit hole!

PERCEPTION

We do not perceive reality as it is. Rather, perception is a subjective construct of the mind. It all starts with sensory information (sensation): stimuli received by our receptor cells. You might have learned in school, like I did, that we have five senses (sight, hearing, smell, touch, and taste), but we actually have many more senses than that. We can, for example, sense temperature, pain, and our body in space. If we take the example of vision, sensory information from, say, stargazing is about physics: spatial frequency, brightness, orientation, etc. Then the brain is going to make sense of this information by organizing the visual field into something meaningful. We need to quickly understand our environment and recognize a potential threat in no time if we want a chance to survive (better safe than sorry, or dead!). The brain is a powerful pattern recognizer, and it sometimes recognizes patterns that aren't there, like the shape of a saucepan in the stars, for example. The process of creating these meaningful mental representations of the world is what we call perception. Lastly, if you know about the constellation that has the shape of a saucepan, you can then understand that you are looking at Ursa Major. This is "cognition", or access to knowledge. In summary, sensation is about sensory information (physics), perception is about constructing meaningful patterns from it, and cognition is about semantics (knowledge). We might think that this is a strictly serial process that happens in this order (bottom-up), but in reality it's very often a top-down process. This means that your cognition, or your knowledge about the world, is going to influence your perception of it. Take the example of the "save" icon, typically represented by a floppy disk. If you're old enough to have interacted with floppy disks in the twentieth century, then this symbol is immediately meaningful to you. But if you were born after they went out of use, then you had to learn what this weird icon is representing. For a given input (stimulus), we can perceive it differently depending on our prior knowledge, our expectations, the context, and even our culture. We do not perceive reality as it is. Perception is a *construct* of the mind. Therefore, we should not be surprised when others don't perceive things the same way we do.

MEMORY

Memory is the process by which we encode information, store it, and eventually retrieve it. When we encode information, it happens in the memory component that we call "working memory". Working memory (WM) is a short-term memory that allows us to temporarily store (for a few minutes maximum) and process information at the same time. Reading my sometimes long sentences requires information to be processed in your WM, as you need to store the words you are reading at the same time as you're making sense of them. It's also the case if you need to do a mental calculation, solve a problem at work, or play a video game. In our life, working memory is usually the memory system that allows us to accomplish our tasks. Although essential to information processing and encoding, WM is very limited. We cannot process too many things at the same time. For example, you might be able to mentally calculate 57 + 34, but it's much trickier to mentally calculate 817 x 957 because too many elements (items, or digits in this case) need to be held in working memory. WM capacity is not great in adults (about three to four items can be held in working memory simultaneously), and it's even worse in children. And if you try to accomplish another task as you mentally calculate, such as beating a specific rhythm with your foot, you're likely going to be very disappointed with your brain. We cannot efficiently multitask, and we are mostly unaware of this. Working memory is taking care of what we call "executive functions". It's controlling and managing our attention resources so that we can reason, make decisions, and accomplish complex cognitive tasks. When we attempt to multitask, we are never as efficient as we are when doing one task at a time. We might get away with multitasking when we accomplish two tasks that do not require much attentional resources and are quite automatic, such as walking while singing a song we know by heart. But anytime one of those tasks (or both) requires more attention, we are likely to take more time to accomplish both tasks when we divide our attention than if we fully focus on one task, and we are also more likely to make more mistakes within both tasks. In reality, we are usually switching our attention between tasks rather than truly doing them at the same time. In this sense, efficient multitasking is mostly a myth. You might have experienced it if you ever were distracted by your baby crying while you were cooking, and as you were taking care of your baby, you forgot that you were in the middle of boiling eggs when you got interrupted, until they explode. Or if you ever have forgotten where you put your keys because you were doing too many things when you arrived home. When these tasks are benign (such as texting a friend while watching TV), we mostly don't realize our lack of efficiency as we divide our attention in an attempt to accomplish multiple tasks at the same time. However, trying to multitask when engaged in an activity that requires our undivided attention, such as driving, could end catastrophically. We will talk about attention and its limitations in greater detail in the next section.

The other component of memory that I would like to highlight is long-term memory, which is responsible for storing all kinds of information after it is processed by our working memory. We do not currently know the limitations of long-term memory, which mostly means that we don't know how much is too much information for our brain to remember. This doesn't mean that we don't forget information – we do. It means that we sometimes forget information immediately but that we can also remember something for our whole life, and that we do not need to "erase" our "hard drive" in order to make space in our mind to learn new things. The brain is not a computer, so we could potentially keep learning and remembering new information. Long-term memory has two main components, which store different types of information: explicit memory and implicit memory. Explicit memory, also called "declarative memory", relates to all information that you can retrieve consciously and which you can talk about ("declare"). It's the memory of general facts about the world (e.g. the name of European capitals) and about personal events (e.g. what you did last night). By contrast, implicit memory mostly relates to actions (procedural memory): how to ride a bike, drive a car, dance, draw, etc. Overall it seems that implicit motivation is more robust than explicit memory. Once you've learned how to ride a bike or drive a car, it usually takes longer to forget than facts and events. This is why it can take you a while to get used to first looking to the right when you cross the street if you're a New Yorker visiting London (and vice versa). Habits die hard, as we say. It's quite difficult to go against our automatic behavior, and our "muscle" memory (procedural memory) is strong.

Implicit memory is also involved in conditioned responses. Conditioning is a form of implicit learning by which two stimuli are associated over time. Pavlov's dogs learned to associate the sound of a bell with food presentation; therefore, they were conditioned to salivate at the sound of the bell. This is what we call classical conditioning, or Pavlov's conditioning. There's another type of conditioning, called "operant conditioning", whereby we learn that a specific action after the occurrence of a stimulus can lead to a reward (or a punishment). For example, if we hear our car beeping annoyingly as we start driving, we've learned that we need to fasten our seatbelts to make the annoyance stop. You might also have learned your multiplication tables at school through such conditioning: if I say "Three times six?", the number "18" might come to your mind immediately if you're a native English speaker because you've learned through repetition in this specific language that this is the right answer (and because you were congratulated – rewarded – when you responded correctly). We will talk about conditioning again in the section below about motivation.

Human memory is complex and fascinating. One of its main limitations is of course that we forget information over time. In the nineteenth century, the German psychologist Herman Ebbinghaus studied the limitations of our memory in an experiment. He taught himself a list of syllables that did not have any meaning (such as "LEV" or "ZOF") to avoid any familiarity with the content, until he knew them by heart. And then he varied the moment he had to recall all these syllables and measured his performance. The results are shown in Figure 1.2. After only 20 minutes, he forgot about 40% of the content learned, and after a day, he forgot close to 70% of the content (Ebbinghaus, 1885). This result, which was replicated (reproduced) in modern days, means that when we learn non-meaningful content, we are likely to lose 70% of it from one day to the next. Hopefully tomorrow you will remember more than 30% of the information you read in this book today! You likely will, given that the content of this book is not gibberish to you (at least that's my intent). Even though this "forgetting curve" represents a worst-case scenario (learning

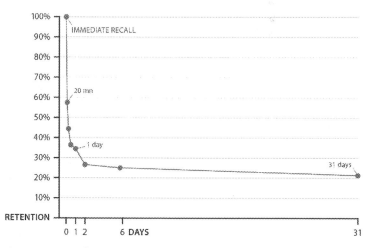

Figure 1.2 The forgetting curve (based on Ebbinghaus, 1885)

non-meaningful content), it's important to remember that our memory is error prone.

Not only do we forget a lot of information as time passes but also what we remember can often be altered, especially information stored by our declarative memory (facts and personal events). We can even recall a memory that actually never happened (false memory bias)! Just as cognition influences our perception, it also influences our memory. And if we can consider perception to be a construct of the mind, memory is a re-construction. Memory does not work like a tape recorder; it constantly encodes, decodes, and re-encodes information, which introduces a lot of errors and biases. In research studying the reliability of eyewitness testimonies, Loftus and Palmer (1974) demonstrated that our souvenirs can be influenced simply by the way we ask questions about them. In this study, participants had to watch a video of car accidents. In one condition, participants were later asked to estimate by memory when asked this question: "How fast were the cars going when they hit each other?" In another condition, participants were asked the same question with the only change being the verb: "How fast were the cars going when they smashed each other?" Depending on the verb used in the question ("hit" versus "smashed"), participants evaluated (as they were remembering the video they saw) the speed of the car differently. Participants in the "smash" condition estimated that the cars were going faster on average (10.46 mph) than did participants in the "hit" condition (8 mph), and this difference was statistically significant. In addition, a week later, the same participants were asked (without watching the video again) if they remembered seeing broken glass on the scene of the accident (there was none). About twice as many participants in the "smash" condition falsely remembered seeing broken glass than did participants in the "hit" condition. The impact of a single word on our memory is quite startling, and it raises concerns on the validity of eyewitnesses' memory (and anyone's). It also explains why it's important to build survey questions very carefully, to avoid biasing answers (e.g. by avoiding leading questions).

Our memory, just like the rest of the brain, has great capacity but also great limitations, which we need to be mindful of. We forget information, and what we remember can be altered. One of the ways to improve our memory is by focusing our attention when we process information in working memory. The deeper you process information, the better the long-term retention. Remembering information efficiently starts with encoding it carefully. Therefore, in many cases, learning by doing is more efficient than learning by reading, for example, because when you accomplish an action you are often more likely to process information in a deeper way. So I would encourage you to share all the things you are hopefully learning in this book with someone else, using your own words. This would be a way to manipulate information profoundly and therefore remember it better.

ATTENTION

Attention allows us to focus our information-processing resources on a small amount of stimuli among all the ones reaching our senses continuously. In the section about memory, we've already explained the need to allocate attention to process information in working memory. Attention can either be active (top-down) or passive (bottom-up). Active attention is a controlled process whereby we direct our attention to a certain task, such as reading this book. Passive attention is a process whereby something in the environment triggers an attentional response, such as suddenly hearing your partner asking you a question as you were reading your book, thereby requiring you to redirect your attention. Attention can also be selective (focused) or divided (what we commonly call multitasking). When we are focusing on a specific task (selective attention), we filter out all irrelevant information. For example, at a loud work party, we focus our attention on what our colleague is telling us by filtering out the rest of the conversations around us. If we suddenly hear someone close by pronounce our name in a separate conversation and we realize it's the voice of our boss, we might want to try to listen to both conservations at the same time (divided attention). As we saw when talking about the limitations of working memory, this usually doesn't go well. We are likely not able to process what our colleague is telling us so we can focus more on what our boss is saying, probably resulting in our colleague realizing something is off and asking us if we're listening. We are really bad at multitasking, and it gets worse the more complex or new one or both tasks are because they then require more attentional resources to accomplish. And this is why we cannot easily pay attention to what's happening in our surroundings, even if it's surprising, when we are focused on a task. You might miss your train stop if you are reading a fascinating book, not notice that your partner is talking to you if you are playing an engaging video game, or not realize that all your colleagues have left the office for the day as you were deeply focused on your work. This is what we call "inattentional blindness" in psychology, and it's very strong.

Just like perception and memory, attention is influenced by our cognition. If we know an activity well, we are usually less easily distracted than when we are unfamiliar with it. And if we train ourselves into doing a task, such as driving a car, at some point it requires less attentional resources to accomplish this task. Once you do not need to pay attention to what your feet and hands need to do to drive, you can allocate the freed attentional resources to navigation. Our attention is heavily limited, and we are mostly unaware of it. Picture attention as the finite resource necessary to information processing. If you allocate all this resource to one specific task, it's ideal. If you divide this finite resource among different tasks, it will very likely be less efficient. When there is too much information to process at the same time or when one task is particularly demanding, we can experience an excessive "cognitive load" that can negatively impact learning, even if we are often unaware of this limitation. It's important to understand that our attentional resources are heavily limited so that we can improve our retention and our overall performance. It's particularly important in education; students need to focus their attention to be able to learn more efficiently. Paying attention pays off!

MOTIVATION

Motivation is very important to understand because it's directing us to accomplish actions. There is no behavior without motivation. You would not be reading this book if you weren't motivated to do so. Maybe you are interested in the topic, or maybe someone has asked you to read it. (I'm saluting my proofreaders here, thanks!) Motivation is very important because when we are motivated to do an activity, we typically pay more attention to it, solve problems better, and retain information more efficiently. The problem is that there are many existing theories about human motivation, and we do not currently have one motivation theory that can explain all our behaviors. For the sake of simplicity, I will focus here on two important types of motivation that have attracted a lot of interest: extrinsic motivation and intrinsic motivation. Extrinsic motivation is when you do something in order to obtain something else (i.e. a reward) extrinsic to the task. Intrinsic motivation is when you do something for the pleasure of doing it, not to get something external to the activity. Let's describe these two types of motivation in greater detail.

Explicit motivation is about how the environment is shaping our behavior. This is overall what behavioral psychologists study. Our everyday behaviors are influenced by rewards (e.g. earning money, winning a badge, gaining loot in a video game, etc.) or "punishments" (e.g. money loss, failure, pain, etc.) we receive from the environment. As we mentioned earlier, this is called operant conditioning: it is when you learn the connection between one stimulus and the probability of getting a reward if you make the appropriate action (e.g. seeing a delicious snack in a vending machine can lead to a near certain pleasurable experience if we put money in the machine and press the correct button, unless the snack gets stuck when it falls). Sometimes the reward arrives late (e.g. solving a math problem in a school exam and getting a good grade from the professor a few days later), sometimes the reward is immediate (e.g. solving the same math problem on an interactive platform and getting a badge right away). The closer in time the reward is to the action, the more efficiently we learn the association. Although conditioning is everywhere in humans and other animals, and helps us survive by seeking pleasure and avoiding pain, it has a bad reputation and is widely misunderstood in the public today. This is mainly because of an infamous behavioral psychologist called B.F. Skinner, who did a lot of research on operant conditioning in the middle of the twentieth century. The typical apparatus that Skinner used to conduct his experiments was an operant conditioning chamber, now called a "Skinner box". An animal (usually a rat or a pigeon) would be isolated in the chamber that contained a food dispenser and a lever. After a specific stimulus occurred (such as a light turning on), if the rat pressed the lever, a food pellet would be delivered into the food dispenser. Skinner discovered that rewarding a specific behavior (giving food if the correct lever is pressed) had a tendency to motivate the rat to increase this behavior (i.e. press this lever more often), while punishing a behavior (giving an electrical shock if the wrong lever is pressed) had a tendency to decrease that behavior. Although our brain is far more complex than the rat's, these results have been generalized to humans.

Conditioning, also called "instrumental learning", is not controversial by itself; it's just an efficient way to learn how to avoid what we consider as undesirable outcomes and how to get more of the rewards we care about. This instrumental learning certainly has a lot of merits and was largely used in the twentieth century in the education, military, and work environments (and still is today). However, it has also been widely criticized because this paradigm ignores important unobservable aspects of learning (such as attention or memory, those mental processes studied by cognitive psychologists), and behaviorism enthusiasts often overlooked undesirable side effects. For instance, punishments can induce stress or aggression and can ultimately be detrimental to learning. Not to mention that stress and anxiety can also damage one's health (rat or human). Skinner used physical punishments to torture the poor rats and pigeons in his lab in the name of science. Even when punishment is not physical (e.g. being publicly shamed for eating a massive steak in the context of the climate emergency), it is not as efficient as learning by being rewarded for the opposite behavior (getting a token of appreciation for choosing the vegan option). Physical punishments have obvious heavy consequences on well-being and are thus clearly intolerable. That being said, we can anticipate that people will generally do more of a certain behavior (i.e. accomplish a task) when it leads to a reward (or at least when it doesn't lead to a punishment) than when it leads to a punishment (or at least when it's not rewarded). This is what extrinsic motivation means in a nutshell. However, since humans are not machines, or rats, we don't always do things to maximize extrinsic rewards.

Intrinsic motivation is when we do an activity or a task for the pleasure of doing it, not to gain something external to the task. You might like to write, draw, play music, or solve math problems even if you're not paid for it. Playing games is typically intrinsic by essence because games are an "autotelic" activity. Its purpose is contained in itself, unless you are playing games professionally (e.g. sports, esports) or to please someone else (such as your kid who wants to play hide-and-seek but you're not really into it). The dominant framework to understand intrinsic motivation is called "self-determination theory" (SDT). This theory posits that we are intrinsically motivated in doing an activity when this activity satisfies our needs for competence, autonomy, and relatedness (Ryan and Deci, 2000). Competence is about feeling in control and a sense of progression. When we learn a new skill (e.g. how to play the piano), if we see ourselves progressing regularly, it's encouraging. When we don't perceive that we are progressing, it can be highly demotivating because we do not feel competent. Autonomy is about self-expression and having meaningful choices. At work, it's usually more motivating to be given an objective and have the autonomy to define how to reach it. Lastly, humans are a very social species, and we need to feel affiliated with others, such as when we feel part of a team. Intrinsic motivation is quite powerful, and sometimes introducing an extrinsic reward for doing an activity we find intrinsically motivating can deter our intrinsic motivation. It depends on many variables, though, and it seems to be mostly the case when those rewards curb our feeling of competence, autonomy, or relatedness. Even if you love your job, you would still dislike not receiving your paycheck at the end of the month! And receiving a raise will be felt not only as an extrinsic reward but also as feedback on our growing mastery (competence). This makes it tricky to clearly distinguish between intrinsic motivation and extrinsic motivation because both often happen in tandem.

One last theory that I would like to highlight here because of its relevance to video games is the "theory of flow". Being "in the flow" means being in a state of deep concentration, when we are totally immersed in and focused on doing an activity that is meaningful to us and that we find intrinsically motivating. It describes the optimal experience whereby a "person's body or mind is stretched to its limits in a voluntary effort to accomplish something difficult and worthwhile" (Csikszentmihalyi, 1990, p. 3). For psychologist Mihaly Csikszentmihalyi, flow is the secret to happiness because he found that people are the happiest when they encounter this sense of optimal experience often in their lives. There are many other theories on motivation and other types of motivation, such as implicit motivation (our impulses, tied to our biology) and motivation tied to our personality. Keep in mind that human motivation is very complex and that we do not well understand why people do the things they do.

EMOTION

Emotion refers to a state of physiological arousal (e.g. accelerating heart rate and sweaty palms) that can also (but not always) involve the cognition (knowledge) related to it (e.g. feeling fear). It's another highly complex topic, and we barely understand how it works and how it influences us. The "limbic system" is generally regarded as the system for emotions, and it involves (but not exclusively) the hypothalamus, the hippocampus, and the amygdala. In a fight-or-flight situation, as in the presence of danger, for example, the hypothalamus will regulate the production of hormones (e.g. adrenaline and cortisol) to raise your awareness and tense your muscles. Meanwhile, the amygdala and the hippocampus "identify" the situation, compare it to older events "stored" in memory, and help store this new event so that we can in the future more efficiently avoid this danger. Keep in mind here, I am simplifying what is happening in the brain.

Most of the time our emotion helps us reason and make the right decisions for our survival. But it can also trick us into making irrational decisions. Let's look at an example. Consider this proposal:

• Would you accept a gamble that offers a 10% chance to win $95 and a 90% chance to lose $5?

Think about whether you would accept this gamble. Now, consider this proposal:

• Would you pay $5 to participate in a lottery that offers a 10% chance to win $100 and a 90% chance to win nothing?

Which proposal would you accept? Both? Only one of them? If so, why? The eminent professor in psychology Daniel Kahneman, who won the Nobel Prize in Economic Science in 2002, explains in his seminal book, *Thinking, Fast and Slow* (2011), that people are more likely to accept the second proposal than the first one because of our strong aversion to loss. For instance, in the first proposal, it makes us think of $5 as a possible loss, whereas in the second proposal, it's framed in such a way to make us think of those $5 as a payment, and this is less painful. Our brain is biased in many ways, and our irrational behavior cannot always be blamed on our emotions. As a matter of fact, Kahneman's work (with Amos Tversky) highlighted that humans commit a lot of systematic errors that can mostly be attributed to the "design of the machinery of our cognition" itself. This sentiment is also expressed in professor in psychology and behavioral economics Dan Ariely's book *Predictably Irrational* (2008): human biases and mistakes are often so systematic that we can reliably predict them.

Even though emotion guides our behavior – sometimes in a detrimental way – as we seek pleasure and we avoid pain, we also know that our cognition can influence our emotion. For example, when we are offered a very well presented dish in a fancy restaurant that has a great reputation, we usually expect to have a good experience, and we are likely to feel more pleasure as we eat this meal than if we eat the same meal on a paper plate at our desk. This is what we call "appraisal" (i.e. judgment). Heightened expectations and aesthetics have a positive impact on appreciation (unless expectations are noticeably later betrayed).

HOW THE BRAIN WORKS: TO SUM UP

The purpose of this chapter was to give you an overview of how our brain works so that we can tackle the psychology of video games. Experiencing a video game (like anything else) happens in our mind, which is why this basic overview, even though highly simplified, is an important foundation for the rest of the book. To sum up, when we process information and learn, it generally starts by perception of certain stimuli from the environment. We "process" this information in our working memory, which requires attentional resources. Then, we "store" information in long-term memory. Factors like how focused we are in doing a task (attention), our motivation to accomplish it, and the emotions associated will have an impact on information processing and long-term retention (as well as other factors that we didn't mention here).

Remember that the brain is extremely complex. We are barely scratching its surface (so to speak), and it remains quite mysterious for the most part. Therefore, be wary of sensational headlines about the brain. As Carl Sagan would say, "extraordinary claims require extraordinary evidence". Many myths are circulating, such as "We only use 10% of the brain", "There are right brain versus left brain activities", or "Rewards give us addictive dopamine shots". Those claims are either false (such as the first one – we use all of our brain) or grossly exaggerated to the point that they are not accurate anymore. In fact, for any activity, both hemispheres of our brain are collaborating, so it is wrong to say that the right hemisphere is "creative" while the left hemisphere is "analytical". Also, dopamine (like other brain chemicals) has many purposes (such as being critical to movement), and it spikes (i.e. we get a "shot") when we gain a reward that was not expected, not when the reward is obtained as expected. So fast release of dopamine doesn't happen when we get a reward but when we gain an *unexpected* one. At least this is one of the things we understand from dopamine so far. The way brain chemicals work is like everything else about the brain: extremely complex. While the brain is fascinating and discoveries are made every day, there's also a lot of "neurobullshit" circulating.

2

GAME USER EXPERIENCE

How do we use psychology when creating video games? Before answering this question, I need to digress once again so that I can explain what "user experience" is, otherwise known as "human-centered design".

HUMAN FACTORS AND ERGONOMICS

Allow me to take you back to World War II. Back then, highly trained pilots could still make what seemed avoidable fatal errors when flying planes. Under the stress of war, the urban legend says that pilots could confuse the ejection release with the throttle, or the landing gear with flap handles. At the time, the main mindset was to build machines such as warplanes with an engineer-centered approach, in other words, to facilitate the engineering work. The expectation was then to train the humans to fit the system. As a result, in the example of warplanes, cockpits across aircraft models were not consistent and control configurations were creating problems. Therefore, even highly trained humans were making costly mistakes. So the mindset started to shift. Instead of trying to fit humans to operate machines, machines can be designed in such a way to fit human capabilities, performance, and limitations. And this is how the "human-centered design" approach started to flourish. In order to create human-centric technology, the field of human factors psychology and ergonomics is solicited and comprises multiple disciplines, such as psychology and physiology. In a nutshell, the main objective is to make products safer and easier to use by accounting for physical ergonomics (e.g. physical fatigue when we operate machines) as well as cognitive ergonomics (i.e. limitations of our mental processes, such as perception, attention, or memory, as we saw in Chapter 1). When computers started to enter people's homes in the 1980s, a new branch emerged: human-computer interaction (HCI), which has an established set of laws and principles that can be applied to improve digital environments such as a website or . . . a video game for humans using them. The main objective of HCI is to make computerized interfaces and systems more easy and pleasurable to use. However, it doesn't account for the whole experience people will have with a given product, from the first time they hear about it all the way to contacting customer support when an issue arises. The term "user experience" (UX) was thus proposed in the 1990s by Donald Norman – a famous designer and author of the seminal book *The Design of Everyday Things* (2013) – to account for the entire experience a user has with a product and its ecosystem (marketing, website, customer service, etc.). Thus, UX includes having a holistic approach and a global strategy in a company or a development team.

THE UX MINDSET

While HCI is a field of research at the intersection of many disciplines, UX is best described as a mindset. User experience is about shifting from our creator perspective when we participate in developing a product (and its ecosystem) to adopt the perspective of our target audience, the users, in all we do. We "fight for the users", in a sense. The UX approach considers what experience users will have when they interact with a product: Can they easily accomplish their goals? and Is their experience with the product pleasurable? So the main focus is the ease of use (usability) and the pleasure of use (what Don Norman calls "emotional design", 2005). But UX doesn't stop there. It's also considering the whole journey people have with a product, system, or service: how they first hear about it and what expectations they get, their experience in the physical store or the online store, their experience as they unbox the product or download and install it, their interaction with the product itself, their interaction with customer support or community managers should the case arise, etc. UX is considering all of this. Thus, UX is the concern of everyone on a product development team, and everyone in a company should have a UX mindset.

Although the notion of UX is gaining traction, it's still often misunderstood. Some people are narrowing down UX to "user interface" (UI), which is also sometimes narrowed down to how good an interface looks. The position of "UX designer" is becoming popular, which is great news, but I've seen this term creating confusion about what a UX designer is actually doing. Are these people responsible for designing the experience of a product? Well, no, because as we mentioned earlier, the experience of a product is what happens in people's minds. So, by definition, this is not something that can be designed. However, we can design for an experience, which means that we design a system or an environment in the hope that users will have a specific (and good) experience when interacting with it. And everyone is responsible for this, not just UX designers. What UX designers are mostly designing are the interactions and the information architecture, which are very important. For example, how should people interact with a system to buy plane tickets, and what information should we display where in order to make their experience as frictionless and pleasurable as possible? UX designers draw sketches and create prototypes, guided by HCI principles, and then they refine their designs with users' feedback. Perception is subjective, and the experience doesn't lie in the design but in people's minds instead. UX design therefore needs to be an iterative process (which we also call "design thinking", a design methodology with a problem-solving approach). Designs are tested, then redefined based on the findings, and then tested again; this goes on and on until the design accomplishes its targeted functionality, or until the design team goes over budget or runs out of time. User researchers are the experts testing the product during its development and even after it's launched. They can potentially test everything that users will perceive and interact with, not just the work of UX designers. "User research" is another term that can be confusing because it gives the impression that users are the ones studied. They are not. It's the product that is studied. User researchers research the product with the help of a small sample of users who are representative of the target audience (factoring in its diversity). This is how we can check if the experience these people are having as they interact with the product (or its ecosystem) is, indeed, the one we intended for them and if they are having a usable, pleasurable, accessible, inclusive, and safe experience. If not, we try to identify what the issues are and, more importantly, why they are happening and how to efficiently fix them.

It's important to understand that having a UX mindset means placing the humans first, not the business. So ethical considerations are also a critical part of a UX approach. Of course, having a UX culture means aligning product development, support teams, and the executive team (which should define the company values and a code of ethics). If a product is a flop and no one is using it or if it's not economically sustainable, it's pointless; a UX approach also has to consider business goals. However, some business, marketing, or design decisions can sometimes result in increasing revenues but to the detriment of users' best interests. When this happens, the UX mindset is betrayed and lost. Having a UX mindset is about building human-centered technology, not a business-centered one. The philosophy is that if the product is satisfying its target audience, makes sense economically, and is respectful of users, then business goals will be reached. It's a win-win approach. We will talk about ethical considerations in more detail in chapter 5.

All in all, UX should be the concern of everyone in a company as it considers the whole journey users will have with a given product, system, or service. Anytime you've interacted with an object, a website, or an application and you didn't easily understand how to accomplish your goals, you've experienced UX issues. Anytime you've felt that barriers were preventing you from accessing a product, you've experienced UX issues. Anytime you've felt frustrated or annoyed with a product, you've experienced UX issues. And anytime you've felt that you were disrespected as a user or a customer because your personal data was not protected, or you unwillingly subscribed to a paid service and you realized this after the fact, you've experienced UX issues. UX practitioners are trying to anticipate all these issues from happening and are then tracking them down using the scientific method (user research). They work with everyone else to eliminate these issues as much as possible, given the constraints of the system, the budget, the time, and the resources they have. This means that offering the perfect user experience rarely happens, but priorities should be defined and tradeoffs should be made having a UX mindset.

GAME USER EXPERIENCE: THE PSYCHOLOGY BEHIND MAKING GAMES

Game user experience is about having a UX mindset applied to games. Games, including video games, are a bit different from other products. They are not a tool. We don't interact with a video game to accomplish goals that are external to the game itself. Games are an autotelic activity: their purpose is self-contained. We interact with them for the pleasure of interacting with the system. Therefore, although usability considerations are still very important, the pleasure of use is not just nice to have, it's mandatory. A game can be usable, yet if it's boring and not fun to play, we're not going to interact with it. And to be fun to play, games need to have some friction points, unlike other products: we like games that challenge our physical or mental skills, challenge our perception, and/or move us emotionally. Games can challenge perception, like the puzzle game *Monument Valley* (developed by ustwo games), based on the universe of M.C. Escher, an artist who was also challenging people's perception with his art. They can more specifically challenge long-term memory, when players have to remember a specific clue or a recipe, for example, in *Minecraft* (developed by Mojang Studios). And they can more specifically challenge working memory and attention, for example, in time-management games like *Diner Dash* (developed by Gamelab) or racing games like *Mario Kart* (Nintendo). Games can also frustrate you and therefore elicit negative emotions. You might lose a game, experience setbacks, feel lost in a puzzle or a maze, etc. In game UX, unlike UX for many other products, we do not track down all possible frustrations and friction points players (users) can experience. We track down the friction points that are *not* by design. Besides this particularity, game UX has otherwise the same approach, principles, methodology, and philosophy than general UX. However, it's an extremely new approach in the game industry. It's only in the early 2010s that game studios started to talk about UX in a more systemic way and hire for UX positions. Today, UX in the game industry is still viewed as something that can be "done" at some point, late in the development process, rather than being seen as a mindset that should guide everyone at every step of the process. It's also very commonly restricted to UI design or UX design. There aren't as many resources in game UX as there are in more general UX. Therefore, what I will describe here is my own perspective and game UX framework (see Hodent, 2017). Keep in mind that game UX will evolve and hopefully more research and frameworks will enrich the field. In the meantime, take my perspective with a grain of salt.

Game UX can be defined as the approach that considers what experience players will have with a game (and its ecosystem): how they will perceive the game and interact with it, and the emotions and engagement elicited from this interaction, relative to the design intentions. For example, although fear is typically not an emotion we want users to have, it could be relevant in the context of a horror game. There is no one recipe for developing fun games, but having a UX mindset provides ingredients that can be used to make up a specific recipe, depending on what the game is about. Game UX goes beyond the interaction with the game itself and needs to account for the entire player journey, just like with general UX. I will, however, focus more specially on the interaction with the game itself here.

The first important thing we need to do when we develop a game is to define exactly what experience we want to offer and who our target audience is (users). Defining the experience entails determining the main pillars of the game. For example, Fortnite (Epic Games) is a game with building, crafting, and combat as main gameplay pillars. We also need to define where we want to challenge players. Fortnite challenges attention, reflexes, coordination with teammates, and strategic planning, for example. It is not a game that challenges perception or long-term memory for the most part (of course games challenge all our mental processes, but more or less substantially). Designing a game means making countless decisions and tradeoffs throughout the development process. No game has a perfect UX, but games that stay true to the experience they are supposed to offer are usually more fun and interesting. This is why tradeoffs that will inexorably need to be made should make sense according to the experience intended. Knowing who is the target audience is also critical because perception is subjective; depending on what games people play, they are not used to the same conventions. For example, players who play a lot of shooter games on console know which buttons are typically used for aiming and shooting, which might not be the case for a mobile puzzle game player. Defining the target audience is also important for UX research, as we need to ask players representative of our target audience to play the game so that we can find the relevant issues to solve for them.

Once the audience and the experience are defined (typically during the conception stage), the development team starts what we call the "preproduction" stage, which is basically the main prototyping phase. From this phase on (then there is production, alpha, beta, launch, and post-launch phases), we try to anticipate then fix all frustrations and friction points players may experience with the game that are not by design, while offering the most engaging and fun game possible that stays true to the design and artistic intentions. To guide game developers, I've been using two main game UX pillars as a framework: usability and what I call "engage-ability".

USABILITY

Usability is about the ability of the game to be used, which entails taking into account the human brain limitations in terms of perception, attention, and memory, which we described in Chapter 1. Usability is a well-known UX pillar, and very precise guidelines have been established throughout the years in industrial design and digital product design. The most renowned list of usability heuristics (i.e. rules of thumb) was put together by Jakob Nielsen. In my game UX framework, I've adapted these heuristics to be more "usable" to game developers who have their own vernacular. These game usability heuristics are as follows:

- **Signs and feedback:** this category encompasses all the stimuli that can be perceived by players, including the feedback from their input (for example, the animation of the character moving forward is feedback from the player's input on the thumbstick).
- **Clarity:** the signs and feedback need to be clearly perceived. Since perception is subjective, the most important elements are tested to ensure that they will be perceived as intended by our target audience.
- **Form follows function:** we ensure that the most important elements in the game will be intuitively understood; therefore, we think about how the visual and audio forms of an element will intuitively inform players on its functionality. For example, the enemy character Bowser in the *Super Mario* franchise (Nintendo) has spikes on its back: this informs players that they will likely get hurt if they try to jump on it.
- **Consistency:** consistent signs and feedback help players understand the game and have correct expectations. For example, if the first door encountered can be opened, players will expect all doors to work the same way. If that's not the case in the game, doors that cannot be opened should look different (have a different form) to express its different function.
- **Minimum workload (cognitive and physical load):** there are a lot of stimuli to process in a video game, although our attention

resources are scarce. Therefore, we try to minimize as much as possible the cognitive workload so that we can focus on where we specifically want to challenge the players' attention and memory. For example, in *Fortnite*, every time a player is approaching a searchable object, the key to press to search the object is displayed. Players don't have to remember it. We also try to reduce the physical load; how many buttons players need to press to accomplish an action, especially when it's a common action.

- **Error prevention and recovery:** to err is human, so we try to prevent errors that are not part of where we challenge players, and when an error occurs, we try to help players recover from it. For example, showing a confirmation screen before the player is about to destroy a rare item to get raw material back is error prevention. Offering an "Undo" button when the player realizes after the fact that they actually needed the item they have just destroyed is error recovery.

- **Flexibility and accessibility:** we must strive to offer various options – such as remapping of controls, subtitles, or color-blind mode – so that everyone can play. A game should be accessible, which means that it should not contain unnecessary barriers to enjoy it.

The goal of these guidelines is to ensure that the game is going to be as intuitive and easy to use as possible. We work to remove all frustrations players might experience that are not by design.

ENGAGE-ABILITY

Offering good usability is critical for any product, including games, yet a game can be easy to use and boring. We typically interact with games solely for the pleasure of playing them. Thus, if a game is not engaging, it's completely defeating its purpose. Don Norman speaks of "emotional design" (2005) to highlight the importance of any product to be more than just about functionality. But for games this emotional design is not merely important; it's the whole point. Game developers often talk about "fun" or "immersion". "Fun" is a good term, but the problem is that many people have a different perspective of what they find fun. Given that the purpose of a framework is to be understood by the whole team, I prefer to use the term "engagement" and to refer to the ability of the game to be engaging, as it's a more objective concept to break down. Engage-ability (which is a made-up word for lack of a better term) is a much fuzzier concept than usability, since we don't fully understand why people do the things they do. Therefore, there aren't any solid guidelines to achieve engage-ability yet. Throughout my work at Ubisoft, LucasArts, and Epic Games, there were three pillars I considered in order to improve the engage-ability of a game: motivation, emotion, and game flow.

MOTIVATION

We do not accomplish any action unless we are motivated to do so. Thus, motivation is at the core of engage-ability. However, like we saw in Chapter 1, countless theories of human motivation exist, and we currently do not have any motivational theory that can account for all of human behaviors. Among the different types of motivation, we usually focus on two that are the most applicable to games: extrinsic and intrinsic motivation. As a quick reminder, extrinsic motivation is when you do something in order to get something that is external to the task. It's when, for example, you wait in the queue to get into a ride at the fair. Waiting in line is a means to an end. Video games often master extrinsic motivation: players need to accomplish quests or actions, or harvest many resources in order to obtain a specific reward. Precise goals, and clear rewards associated with these goals, are very important to make a game engaging because they allow for player strategy. For example, in a role-playing game (RPG), there might be a specific quest that you want to do, but your avatar (i.e. the character you control) is currently too weak to participate. So you establish your strategy in order to develop your avatar and equip it with the appropriate skills and abilities that you will need to accomplish your goal. Extrinsic motivation is important to account for but is not enough. Game developers also need to account for intrinsic motivation, which is our motivation to do certain things just for the pleasure of doing them. Self-determination theory (SDT) is the theory commonly used to accomplish this, which boils down to trying to satisfy players' need for competence, autonomy, and relatedness. Competence being mainly about having a sense of progression, this progression can be skill-based (e.g. getting increasingly skilled at building fast) or not (e.g. leveling up and buying new skills that make us artificially more powerful within the game). If we do not feel that we are progressing when we engage with an activity, such as learning how to play guitar or trying to lose weight, we are very likely to abandon that activity. This is why progression bars are so compelling. It's not only because of the promise of getting a reward once we reach a new level, it's also because we can see ourselves progressing towards a goal and becoming increasingly competent. It's the same with games.

Autonomy is mainly about self-expression. Being able to choose your skins, your dance moves, or how you can overcome obstacles allows you to feel more autonomous. Sandbox games (e.g. Minecraft or Grand Theft Auto V) and games offering a lot of cosmetic options (when these options are meaningful to players) are often engaging because they are satisfying players' autonomy.

Lastly, relatedness is about having meaningful relationships with other people in a game. Humans are a very social species, and multiplayer games often offer compelling relatedness. This can be either through competition or cooperation. Although cooperation is often more engaging, which is why most competitive games offer cooperative options (e.g. playing in a squad or playing in a team against another team).

EMOTION

Emotion in games is mainly about what we call "game feel" and about offering new content. Game feel refers to how good it feels to interact with a game. It's about its camera, controls, and characters (often called "the 3Cs"). It's about the sense of presence, provided by an

AI (artificial intelligence) that reacts adequately to what players are doing, a meaningful story, or great music, among many other things. Lastly, it's about the physical reality of the game, how believable it is (rather than its photo-realism). I won't get into any detail here, but emotion is also about the surprises and novelties that are offered to players. When players don't get something new every now and then (new characters, maps, or events), they typically get bored and leave the game to play something else. Online games constantly need updates, new campaigns, modes, skins, or seasons to meet players' expectations, which often makes it hard for the development team to keep up, and they typically end up doing overtime regularly.

GAME FLOW

Game flow comes from the concept of "flow" investigated by psychologist Mihaly Csikszentmihalyi (1990). As he was trying to find out the secret to happiness, he noticed that those who were happier in life experienced the state of flow more often. Like we mentioned in Chapter 1, you're in a state of flow when you are deeply concentrated in doing an activity that is both worthwhile to you and challenging. You can experience this state at work, when being creative (e.g. if you like to draw, knit, or play music), and when you play certain video games. Jenova Chen is a game designer who has extensively explored the notion of game flow through games like *Flow*, *Flower*, or *Journey* (developed by thatgamecompany). One of the main components of game flow is challenge. A game needs to have the right level of difficulty so that the game is never too easy (otherwise we get bored) or too hard (otherwise we get too stressed). That's the main difference between the UX of a game and the UX of other products: in games we generally need to challenge the user. As we already mentioned several times, game developers are carefully implementing frictions that are by design: players are going to encounter obstacles they will need to overcome. For instance, multiplayer games need to perfect their matchmaking so that players at the same level of expertise and skills are matched together. Neither being destroyed in no time nor winning too easily is fun. Game flow is also about pacing: the rhythm of stress and pressure. A game typically has some intense moments and more relaxing ones. Many action games have "waves of enemies", for example, and in "battle royale" games, players have relatively calmer moments to prepare, alternated with moments when encounters are getting inevitable as the map is shrinking. Last but not least, "onboarding" is paramount to game flow. In order to enter a state of flow while playing a game, you need to understand its rules and how to succeed (or at least how to get better at playing). Onboarding players properly, through elegant tutorials that feel part of the game, will greatly impact the feeling of immersion because it allows players to efficiently learn to be competent in playing the game. Sure, they will make mistakes and probably die a few times, but if the game allows them to understand what happened and how to get better next time, they will be able to progress. Having a sense of progression is one of the main pillars of intrinsic motivation, as explained earlier.

A SCIENTIFIC APPROACH TO SOLVING PROBLEMS

We have seen so far how psychology helps in making games: knowledge from cognitive psychology (and overall cognitive science) and human factors psychology is offering guidelines to provide the best experience possible to players in terms of usability (ease of use) and engage-ability (fun). One last element we need to talk about is how we identify UX issues and their origins. Solving problems is relatively easy. Finding and solving the right problems is what is difficult, as Don Norman often says. And since humans are biased, relying on the gut feeling of different members of the game team, all having their own subjective perception, scarce attention, and fallible memory, can lead to costly setbacks. This is why it is important to rely on the scientific method to identify and prioritize issues. I will more specifically focus here on experimental methods allowing us to establish knowledge, solve a problem, or answer a question in a systemic way, using a precise procedure defined beforehand. This is what we call a "hypothetico-deductive" model of reasoning, whereby a measurable effect is collected and analyzed using a standardized protocol in order to confirm or disprove a hypothesis. Experimental psychology uses such a method.

This is what UX researchers do: they use the scientific method to pose hypotheses with the game team, design experimental protocols accordingly, and then gather and analyze data while removing as many human biases as possible. Among the tools that game UX researchers use are "playtests". During these tests, a small sample of users representative of the target audience (typically around eight participants) is invited to help identify issues the game has, preferably in a UX lab. They can be asked to do a specific task, such as finding an item in the game inventory and craft it, either using an early version of the game or a prototype version. When the development of the game is more advanced, we often ask participants to simply play the game as if they were at home. UX researchers then observe what participants are doing and document all the times participants made mistakes, took a long time to figure something out, or missed important information. These observation phases are usually followed by surveys that participants fill out. Since we know that surveys should not have leading questions (see Chapter 1) or influence respondents in any way, they are crafted carefully. Typically, very precise and objective questions are asked in these surveys, such as showing a picture of an icon from the game and asking participants what they believe it represents.

In the early stages of the development of the game, it's mostly usability that is tested. Once critical systems are implemented in the game, engage-ability can also be tested, although it's arguably much more difficult. But we can ask questions to find out if participants are looking forward to completing a specific goal, if they know what they can do with the rewards they received, if they feel that they are progressing in the game, if they think they have meaningful choices, or if they believe the game is more fun to play with others (in the case of multiplayer games). These questions around motivation can help identify if there is a clear weakness in the game. Many modern games today have a phase of "closed beta". This is when the game is nearly finished but is still being polished and balanced, and a much larger sample of players (such as a few thousand) can be invited to access the game early and test it from home, and they can sometimes be asked to answer questions in online surveys.

Another tool that is used in UX research is "analytics". Analytics is an umbrella term covering the collection of telemetry data and making sense of it. This tool is also vastly used by what we call the "business intelligence" team, focused on supporting business decision making, and is very trendy in the technology industry. A lot of aggregated data are collected when we use apps, navigate the Internet, or play games. The main business purpose of using game analytics, especially with free-to-play games, is to check how many people are playing the game each day (which is called "daily active users"), what proportion of players come back the next day, the next week, or a least once during the month (which is called "retention"), if on the contrary they quit the game definitively (which is called "churn"), and how many players are buying something in the game (which is called "conversion"). When used in game UX research, analytics is more about answering questions like "Where are players dying?" "Are they getting stuck somewhere?" "Is the game correctly balanced, or is a hero or weapon overpowered or underpowered?" etc. Of course the retention rate (how many players are coming back to play) is an interesting metric because a fun game is typically a game we want to come back to. So if the retention rate is poor, it obviously means that the game is not appreciated. But beyond this consideration, it's not really a useful metric for game UX, as we care about more granular elements. Just like with playtests, game analytics can help us track down issues players might encounter. For example, if data shows that only a small percentage of players are using a specific feature in the game, we're going to start investigating why, especially if this feature is important to the enjoyment of the game. The strength of analytics is to help us understand *what* players are doing as they play at home, outside the constraints and biases of a UX lab, but it's often not good at explaining *why* because quantitative data lack context. Therefore, UX researchers sometimes partner with data analysts and use mixed-method research to combine quantitative data with qualitative user research in an effort to have a better understanding of the main issues the game has.

The scientific method allows the game development team and UX practitioners to identify the most critical UX issues, understand why they are occurring, and hopefully fix the right problems so that the game can offer a better experience.

GAME UX: TO SUM UP

Making games is hard, and many projects fail. These usability and engage-ability pillars constitute a game UX framework that I find very useful and practical to follow when developing a game, as shown in Figure 2.1. It can be used as a checklist to identify the most critical issues to fix, as well as the missing features or elements in the game to reach its full potential. There is no known recipe for fun and successful games, but this framework offers ingredients that we know are key to craft usable and engaging games. Game makers can use these ingredients, informed by psychology, to make their own

GAME USER EXPERIENCE

❑ Signs & Feedback
❑ Clarity
❑ Form Follows Function
❑ Consistency
❑ Minimum Workload
❑ Error Prevention & Recovery
❑ Flexibility & Accessibility

USABILITY

❑ Motivation
competence, autonomy, relatedness meaningful goals & rewards

❑ Emotion
game feel, presence, surprises

❑ Game flow
difficulty curve, pacing, learning curve

ENGAGE-ABILITY

Figure 2.1 A game UX framework (from Hodent, 2017)

successful recipe, depending on the kind of experience they want to offer and on the audience they are making the game for.

A game UX mindset is about considering players first. It entails ensuring that the game will be accessible, inclusive, safe, and overall ethical. We briefly talked about accessibility in the usability section. The "U" in UX should account for all users, including disabled players. Games are for everyone, and many unnecessary barriers are sadly preventing some players from playing certain games. It also means that all users from the target audience (mostly defined by what games those players like to play) should feel welcome. Diversity and inclusion (and accessibility that is part of it) still have a long way to go, in games and in game studios alike. Ethics are also often not carefully considered in many studios, although the relatively new free-to-play business model is raising overall more ethical concerns than traditional premium games (that you need to first pay to play). The hope is to see the importance of these topics heightened with the game UX mindset increasing in popularity. There is one topic for which the game industry is relatively more advanced than the rest of the tech industry (especially compared to social media): it's regarding how to keep players safe from antisocial behaviors in online multiplayer games (that can be felt as toxic by those who are the victims of it) as much as possible. Antisocial behavior can be, for example, a player verbally harassing other players or trolling them. Players don't play games to get harassed, and when it happens, it definitely is a bad experience for the victims, so this is a UX issue that needs to be given high priority. Game developers can educate players on how to be respectful to others, for example, by establishing a code of conduct shown to players before they can play the game. Developers can also enforce this code of conduct, for example, by banning players who have been reported as violating the code from playing the game for a few days. Lastly, and more efficiently, the game can be designed in such a way to ensure that antisocial behaviors will not be rewarded. And this is where behavioral psychology comes into play. We know a behavior that is rewarded or not punished will have a tendency to increase, while a behavior that is punished or not rewarded will have a tendency to decrease (operant conditioning, see Chapter 1). With this is mind, we can design games in such a way that antisocial behaviors will either not be possible at all, or at least not rewarded when they are possible. For example, not having a voice chat capability in a multiplayer game (and having instead other tools to allow player collaboration) makes verbal abuse impossible. Another example, this time to illustrate how not to reward antisocial behaviors, would be to rethink certain game rules. Game designer Jenova Chen explained in his talk at the Game UX Summit 2019 that when he was developing with his team the game *Journey* (thatgamecompany) on Sony PlayStation 3, he wanted to allow for genuine social connections. They created situations where two players could meet online in the game and collaborate without being able to communicate verbally. The game world is vast, mysterious, and quite harsh, and the game does not explain to players what they can do together; they have to figure it out. The hope was that players would feel vulnerable in this world and thus willing to have a genuine social connection with the other player, collaborate, and try to find a way out together. But when Chen was testing the game in its early stages, he was horrified to see that players, instead of, for example, collaborating to climb up a cliff, would sometimes push the other off a cliff and let them die. Chen was startled by this trolling behavior and didn't understand why players would be mean to each other rather than try to collaborate. But he later realized that the trolling behavior was *rewarded* by the game: something happens, the other player dies in a pool of blood, while collaborating was not as exciting. This does not mean that humans, given the chance, prefer to hurt someone else rather than collaborate, but this is a virtual space, and players just experiment with what they can and can't do, and they will repeat actions that lead to what they perceive as rewarding. So Chen removed collisions between players in the game (i.e. they could not push each other anymore but could go through each other's avatar), and he rewarded players for being close to one another; in this case, they would get energy and be able to fly. In summary, Chen removed the reward given to a trolling behavior and added a reward to the opposite collaborative behavior.

The way Chen talks about the development of the game demonstrates a genuine UX mindset: shifting from the developer's perspective to adopt players' perspectives and iterating on the game until it offers the experience truly intended (in this case, meaningful social connections). The example illustrates the importance (in games, social media, and also society at large) of accounting for operant conditioning: rewarding or not punishing an antisocial behavior will encourage the perpetrator to keep going, while punishing (not physically, of course) or not rewarding the opposite collaborative behavior will discourage it. Game developers generally control the entirety of the game environment (except in the case of augmented or mixed reality games) and define all the signs, feedback, and rewards the game offers. Anticipating the impact of such elements on players and ensuring it will not be detrimental to them are critical to game UX. Players just should have fun playing a game and be respected, welcome, and safe.

3

CAN PLAYING VIDEO GAMES BE BENEFICIAL?

It is estimated that over two billion people worldwide play video games, and the video game industry generated about 150 billion US dollars in 2019, a global revenue that has been increasing in the past years. With such whopping numbers, the impact of video games is under great scrutiny. Could video games have a negative impact on players' mental and physical health, especially that of children, and could video games positively impact cognitive skills, health, and education? There are many resounding claims on both sides, yet they aren't always supported with great evidence. Overall research findings are often inconclusive or contradictory. Further, what little evidence is available is often based on correlational studies whereby a relationship between two variables does not inform on their causal relationship. Let's imagine this scenario: you are researching sunblock sales in your city (variable A), and you find out that they correlate with ice cream sales (variable B) – both increase and decrease at the same time. Does this mean that using sunblock makes people want to eat ice cream (variable A is causing B)? Or could it be that eating ice cream makes people realize that their skin is getting warm and that they should use sunblock (variable B is causing A)? Or maybe a "confounding variable" could be influencing both other variables, such as the weather (when it's warm, both A and B increase). And sometimes two variables correlate by coincidence. In short, correlation does not equate to causation. Correlational studies can provide interesting information, but they usually require more research to understand the relationship between variables.

Additionally, it is important to point out that "video games" is not a homogenous category. There are many different game genres, from puzzle games to action-packed shooter games to strategy games. Some have violent content, some focus on social connections or gifting, some are narrative-driven, some are sandbox games, and others are contemplative. Some are solo games, or multiplayer games that can be competitive or cooperative or both. It is therefore a bit misleading to talk about the "impact of video games" as if those games were just a big block, just like it is perfunctory to talk about the impact of "screen time", since many activities can be done with a screen (watching a movie, working, reading a book or the news, having a video call with a family member, chatting with a friend, playing games). When news outlets report on studies researching the impact of video games, it is important to look at what sort of games they are talking about. And if you are a parent, it's important to pay attention to what types of games your children are playing and even what modes they prefer playing within those games. For example, Minecraft has a "creative" mode (where players can freely create, like what they would do if they were playing with digital Lego blocks) and a more stressful "survival" mode (where players can get attacked and die), among other modes. Fortnite also has a "creative" mode, a "battle royale" mode (where players compete against each other until only one team or one player is the last survivor), a "save the world" mode (where players collaborate to defeat a zombie invasion, save people, and progress in the game via role-playing game mechanics), and sometimes Fortnite can just be a social space to hang out or watch a concert.

Not all video games are similar, and within each game not all modes are equal. It is therefore important to make these distinctions. With this in mind, let's first look into the benefits of playing video games.

BENEFITS OF PLAY

Before looking into the potential benefits of videogame play, let's remember that playing video games is a playful activity. We know that play is important at all ages to keep our mind sharp. When we play, we allow our brain to experiment with situations that can be new and that are often more complex than situations we otherwise encounter in our life. To play is to learn. During childhood, play is even more critical to healthy development because the brain is maturing and is much more malleable (i.e. has more plasticity) than it is in adulthood. There's a considerable body of research emphasizing the importance of play in child development. Through play, children experiment, explore, and learn. Play has adaptive functions and helps children assimilate reality. What is important, though, is to diversify the types of play, as it allows children to experiment in different ways. Physical play, pretend play, symbolic play (e.g. drawing), social play, or playing a game with rules can each be linked to the development of different skills. For example, physical play is linked to the development of motor skills, while pretend play is linked to the development of language (but not exclusively). Certain games with rules, such as board games with numbers, may promote mathematical abilities. Children learn through unstructured free play, adult-guided play, and playing games. As professor of psychology Kathy Hirsh-Pasek and her colleagues point out in their book *A Mandate for Playful Learning in Preschool*, "learning takes place best when children are engaged and enjoying themselves" (2009, p. 3).

Regarding play activities that involve the use of a screen, it is important to note that the American Academy of Pediatrics, since October 2016, recommends that infants avoid all screen media other than video chatting until 18 months old. Early learning primarily happens during interactions with caregivers. Under 2 years of age, children have difficulty relating video material to the real world (this is called the "video deficit") and thus learn better from interacting with an adult than from any video medium. Time spent interacting with a screen is potentially time that is not spent interacting with a human (outside video chatting) and should therefore be avoided. Parents of toddlers aged 18 to 24 months who want to introduce screen media are recommended to engage only with high-quality programming (such as content offered by *Sesame Workshop*) and to accompany their children so they can answer their questions. For children between 2 and 5 years of age, the recommendation is to limit screen time to one hour per day of high-quality programming and to guide children in the activity. For children aged 6 and older, limits are recommended on the use of screen media and especially to ensure that children have enough sleep and physical activity. Although it can be very tricky for parents to assess the quality of the thousands of video games available, they can first check their age rating on the Entertainment Software Rating Board (ESRB) and Pan European Game Information (PEGI) websites, respectively, in North America and Europe. These rating systems do not inform parents whether games are made for a specific age; rather, they inform about some inappropriate content a video game might have that would make it not suitable for children under a specific age (such as violence or gambling). For a content review and age recommendation, parents can check the Common Sense Media website. Checking the content and business model of the games played by children is also recommended. For example, free-to-play games can offer micro-transactions that could be problematic for the youngest. We will talk more about those elements in the next two chapters.

Within the limits of screen time and content recommendations, playing video games should be considered as just another way for children to play and experiment. As long as children's play activity is varied, some video games can be part of that play. But can playing video games offer specific benefits to children and adults?

VISUAL AND COGNITIVE SKILLS

One of the most robust findings of positive effects of videogame play relates to the impact of action games on adults' visuo-spatial and attention skills, such as our capacity to direct our attention to a visual stimulus (visual selective attention). These are typically the skills you need to play action games well, such as first-person shooters (*Call of Duty* series, for example), because you need to quickly track multiple enemies to shoot at them while avoiding getting hurt and, in some cases, helping a teammate. Note that these skills are also needed to drive safely, for example. Some studies have found a correlation between those visual attention skills and playing commercial action games (these studies are mostly conducted with adults, given that many action games have violent content). Action gamers are generally found to have better visual attention skills as compared to non-players. For example, Dye and Bavelier (2010) found that school-age children playing action games showed overall better performance on visual attention tasks as compared to non-players. But these correlational studies cannot really tell us if it's the playing of action games that enhances visuo-spatial skills or if people with good visuo-spatial skills are more inclined to be good at these games and thus play them more because they feel competent (which is important for intrinsic motivation, as we saw in Chapter 1).

Beyond correlational studies, a few interesting experiments have been conducted, whereby participants are trained on a video game and their cognitive skills are measured via a standardized test before (which we call "pre-test") and after ("post-test") the training, as compared to a control group (whose participants play another type of game). This is what we call an "intervention study", or experiment. When participants' performance is enhanced post-test as compared to pre-test in the experimental group but not in the control group, it allows researchers to conclude that it's the video game training that is causing the cognitive enhancement. For example, Green and Bavelier (2003) showed in an experiment that training people on an action video game had an impact on their visual attention skills. In this experiment, participants who didn't play video games were divided into two groups: the experimental group was trained on the first-person shooter *Medal of Honor: Allied Assault* (Electronic Arts) for ten hours (one hour per day for ten days). The control group was trained on the game *Tetris* instead. Before and after training, participants' performance on visual attention tasks, such as their capacity to track multiple moving elements, was evaluated for both groups. The results showed that the group trained on the action game showed an increase of visual attention skills as compared to the control group. If you are more of a *Tetris* than a shooter-game fan, don't be too disappointed! In a training experiment by Okagaki and Frensch (1994), *Tetris* was found to improve spatial ability such as mental rotation time among late adolescents and young adults.

Another experiment, conducted by Li et al. (2009) using a similar protocol (pre-test, training, post-test), showed an increase of visual abilities (i.e. contrast sensitivity) for participants trained fifty hours over nine weeks on action games (*Unreal Tournament* 2004 and *Call of Duty* 2), as compared to a control group trained with a non-action game (*The Sims* 2). Contrast sensitivity is assessed in clinical evaluation of vision, and these results suggest that action video games could be used to improve one's eyesight.

Although training studies are less numerous than correlational studies, they are providing increased evidence that certain games can improve certain visual abilities and cognitive skills. Intervention studies using commercial action games are quite rare with children given that most of these games are not suitable for them. However, there is an interesting one that used the non-violent game *Rayman Raving Rabbids* (Ubisoft) on the Wii console (Nintendo) with children with dyslexia. In this study, Franceschini and colleagues (2013) tested the reading skills of 20 children with dyslexia before (pre-test) and after (post-test) training them for a total of 12 hours. *Rayman Raving Rabbids* is a party game comprising many different mini-games, some action oriented, others less so. Half of the children were trained for twelve hours on one of those action mini-games, while the other half (control group) were trained on a different type of mini-game. The results highlighted that children in the action mini-game group showed improved visual attention skills and reading speed, as compared to those in the control group. These benefits persisted after two months. According to the researchers, this result could be attributed to the fact that visual attention skills are believed to be important for reading acquisition skills.

Research on the cognitive benefits of videogame play is still emerging. For commercial games, findings show that action games (mostly shooters that are usually violent) can have a positive impact on visual attention skills. Other games have been found to yield a positive impact on visual skills and spatial cognition. For other cognitive skills, either no benefits were significantly found or they were found in correlational studies and thus cannot yet be attributed to videogame play since correlation is not causation.

The training studies conducted thus far have shown that a transfer of learning is possible: an ability trained within one context (i.e. playing a game) is transferring onto another similar context (i.e. performance to a standardized test), with effects sometimes lasting months after the video game training. This is quite remarkable because in many cases, training on a certain activity (whether it is a game or not) is making us better at doing only this specific activity. And the large majority of so-called brain training games or "educational" games do just that: train you to perform better at these games (or exercises), and that's it. This is why these training experiment results are promising; transfer of learning to other domains is what education is all about. In this sense, even though we certainly need more research, the potential of certain video games is quite interesting for education. That being said, the transfer observed is generally a "near transfer", whereby the transfer happens on a closely related domain (Sala et al., 2018). So playing action games will not make you "smarter", but they can increase your visual attention over time and the number of objects that you can attend simultaneously, which in turn can improve your performance on similar tasks requiring these skills.

VIDEO GAMES FOR EDUCATION

Educators care that learners acquire new skills that can transfer onto many different situations. An "educational" game should be labeled as such only when we can measure such transfer. However, as you might have guessed, the large majority of commercial educational games cannot truly claim such an outcome (although they do it anyway since we lack a certification process behind the "educational" label). Most of the time, these games aren't even scientifically evaluated to check their impact on players. There are a few exceptions, though, such as the game *ST Math* (*Spatial Temporal Math*) developed by Mind Research Institute. This game introduces mathematical concepts by manipulating virtual objects in space and time, which seems to have a positive impact on mathematics achievement when used at school, as measured by the California Standard Tests (Rutherford et al., 2010). Another example is from Jaeggi and colleagues (2011), who created a working memory task (and a control task) in a graphically rich interactive environment. Elementary and middle school children trained on the working memory task showed gains in fluid intelligence standardized tasks, compared to children trained on the control task. Fluid intelligence refers to the ability to solve problems in new situations that depends on working memory capacity. Interestingly, the children who improved the most were those who rated the training task as challenging but not too challenging, which might remind you of the concept of game flow, important in creating engaging games (see Chapter 2). Lastly, a very recent meta-analysis conducted by Riopel and colleagues (2020) showed that instruction with serious games, compared with more conventional instruction, could be associated with a modest positive effect on science learning achievement.

Besides a few exceptions (in general, carefully crafted by educators and researchers), so-called educational games are usually not genuinely educational. Take the example of games designed to promote literacy skills. In their book *Tap, Click, Read*, Lisa Guernsey and Michael Levine (2015) explain that the push for literacy is not necessarily driven by research on how language and literacy skills develop. Instead, "educational games" are often relying too heavily on ABCs and phonics drills that can sometimes be actually more harmful than truly educational. Too often, apps and games labeled as educational are making unsubstantiated or over-exaggerated claims. And for those that seem to reveal true educational value through standardized scientific evaluation, they might not actually be fun and engaging enough to merit the "game" label. Whether we call them "educational games", "serious games", or "gamification", we often face the same issue: either these "games" aren't truly educational or they aren't fun, or both. Adding cute animations on math exercises and focusing on extrinsic rewards such as badges is certainly not enough to turn something boring into fun. As we saw in Chapter 2, making engaging games is actually pretty hard, even for established game studios with substantial budgets. Game UX is increasingly popular because it provides a framework and ingredients to guide game developers on their difficult journey to craft engaging games. Moreover, "serious games" and "gamification" often have a strong focus on extrinsic rewards. Although operant conditioning (learning to accomplish an action to gain something) is a robust learning paradigm (see Chapter 1), it doesn't transfer very well. Let's say that a game motivates you to exercise every day to get experience points and earn rewards. If one day you stop playing this game, you might also stop exercising regularly. Extrinsic rewards motivate us to do an activity when they keep coming. When they stop, or when we cease to find value in them, we can often stop being motivated. This is why intrinsic motivation is critical to consider in educational games: allowing players to satisfy their need for competence, autonomy, and relatedness. In short, making the activity both playful and meaningful.

The most respected scholars in the field of child development contended that children learn best when they can experiment with the world through play (Piaget, 1962; Vygotsky, 1978). In 1980, mathematician and educator Seymour Papert explained in his seminal book *Mindstorms* that computers could become a powerful educational tool but not by letting the computer instruct the child (like many "serious games" do). Rather, the intent should be to allow children to program the computer so that they can accomplish goals that are *meaningful* to them. Papert developed the Logo computer language at MIT, which, for example, allowed children to draw by using this language. For example, by typing "fd 100" (i.e. forward 100), the cursor (called "turtle") would draw a straight line of 100 units long. To draw a square, children could type "Repeat 4 [fd 100 rt 90]", with "rt 90" meaning "90 degree right turn". Since children like to draw and were excited to use a computer, they discovered on their own, through an iterative trial-and-error process, geometry rules that they needed to instruct the computer to draw what they cared about. For example, if they wanted to draw a house, they first needed to understand the characteristics of a square (four equal sides and four 90 degree angles) to give proper instructions to the computer. This is what we call a "constructionist" approach, whereby we learn by actively constructing our knowledge in a meaningful context. When children develop strategies in playful experiences like these, they seem to be more likely to transfer these strategies to other contexts (Klahr and Carver, 1988).

This idea of letting children construct their knowledge by experimenting within a meaningful and playful context is leading increasingly more educators to use certain commercial games in the classroom, such as Minecraft (developed by Mojang Studios). Minecraft is a very popular "sandbox" game, a procedurally generated world made of blocks, where players can build any object or shape (just like when playing with Lego blocks), and complex machines and systems. Given that many children are engaged with this game and that it offers a lot of possibilities, teachers are leveraging these capabilities in the classroom for a wide range of learning goals (see Lane and Yi, 2017, for an overview). For example, a National Science Foundation–funded research project[1] conducted by an interdisciplinary team of researchers is exploring how Minecraft can generate interest in science. The idea is to let learners interactively explore the scientific consequences of alternative versions of Earth via "What if?" questions in Minecraft. The questions can be "What if the Earth had no moon?" or "What if the Earth were twice its current size?" Thus, the research project is called "What-if Hypothetical Implementations in Minecraft" (or WHIMC). Other popular commercial games have an educational version, such as SimCity (originally designed by Will Wright), whereby players can build and manage cities; Portal (Valve), whereby players solve visuo-spatial puzzles; or Kerbal Space Program (Squad), whereby players build their spaceship through an iterative process using math, physics, and engineering skills. Video games have the potential to invite players to experiment safely with any environment or system. Being so popular, they can also pique children's interest, which in turn can make learning feel effortless because it has a facilitative effect on cognitive functioning, especially attention (see Dewey, 1913; Renninger and Hidi, 2016). And teachers can leverage this power as a tool in their classrooms. Here again, we lack research to truly understand the potential of such commercial and popular games, but it can be argued that teachers and educators remain key in building a meaningful learning environment with these tools.

Another interesting aspect of games for education is that they might reinforce a "growth mindset" (see Dweck, 2006). This refers to considering that intelligence is not a fixed state but a process. Thus, successes or failures are not attributed to being "smart" or "dumb" but to the efforts put into a challenge to overcome. The hypothesis then is that children and adults who have such a mindset understand that increasing competence is more important than performance and that failure is part of the process of learning. Therefore, perseverance should pay. It is usually recommended to avoid celebrating children's accomplishments by telling them that they are smart. Because the day they fail, they might then deduct that they are dumb and that nothing can be done. It's more recommended to celebrate the effort they put into a task so that children can learn to persevere and overcome difficult challenges. Given that many video games confront players with obstacles and failures until they finally win, some researchers are exploring if they can foster a growth mindset. In fact, when we fail in a video game, it is generally associated with trying again, whereas failure in school might make children feel that they are not smart enough. A correlational study suggested that frequent videogame players spent longer trying to solve anagrams and riddles, which they were tested on (and which they could skip), relative to infrequent videogame players (Ventura et al., 2013). More research is needed to explore the potential of video games teaching perseverance, a skill that players could hopefully transfer to other situations.

HEALTH AND WELL-BEING

Using games to promote health, or to prevent or treat diseases, is gaining increasing interest (see Kowert, 2019), and it has a dedicated peer-reviewed journal (*Games for Health Journal*) and conference (Games for Health) focused on this subject. For example, training on action video games has been found to increase the visual acuity of adult patients diagnosed with amblyopia, a sight disorder also called "lazy eye" (Li et al., 2011). A number of studies have also shown that video games can help children understand and even help them manage certain health conditions. For example, a clinical study showed that children and teenagers with diabetes who played a video game on diabetes self-management for six months visited the emergency rooms less often as compared to a control group who played another video game (i.e. pinball game) (Lieberman, 2001). Another well-known game designed for child cancer patients, *Re-Mission*, whereby players shoot cancer cells, significantly improved adherence to treatment protocol and cancer-related knowledge as compared to a control group who played another video game (Kato et al., 2008). A game designed to help children tackle anxiety, *MindLight*, has been effective in reducing levels of anxiety (Schoneveld et al., 2018). This game uses biofeedback, whereby an electrode is placed on the child's forehead to read their brainwaves. In the game, children control a character's movement with a regular controller, and they control a light bubble in the game with their mind. When the child is relaxed and breathes deeply, the light shines brightly; when the child is stressed, the light dimmers and monsters can show up. This game helps children learn to control their anxiety in the safe environment of the game. Although most studies use custom-made games, there is also some evidence that commercial games that satisfy players' needs for competence (self-determination theory of intrinsic motivation), such as *Mario 64* (Nintendo), can foster an increase in self-esteem and a more positive mood after playing, as compared to before playing (Ryan et al., 2006).

Specifically designed video games can benefit health education and physical education among young people. And physically interactive video games (i.e. exergames) can encourage physical exercise (Papastergiou, 2009). Overall, playing video games designed to promote health-related behavior changes lead to many desirable outcomes, from knowledge increases to attitude and behavior changes (Baranowski et al., 2008). One video game designed by Akili Interactive, *EndeavorRX*, became, in June 2020, the first video game approved by the U.S. Food and Drug Administration (FDA) to treat children with attention deficit hyperactivity disorder (ADHD).

The potential of video games to increase the quality of life of older populations is also explored. For example, in a study conducted by Rosenberg and colleagues (2010), senior citizens living in a community showed improvement in subsyndromal depression after only three months of playing *Wii Sports* physical games (Nintendo). Another example, this time using a custom-designed video game (*NeuroRacer*), showed reduced multitasking costs with adults (aged 60 to 85 years old) compared to control groups, with gains persisting for six months (Anguera et al., 2013). Video games might also serve as an interesting tool to combat cognitive decline.

Lastly, some video games allow gamers to help researchers. For example, *Sea Hero Quest* (Glitchers) tests your spatial navigation skills and asks a few questions about you (such as your age). This game has been played by over two million people and helped researchers better understand early signs of Alzheimer's disease as clinicians analyzed all the data collected. Another game, *Foldit*, created in 2008 by researchers at the University of Washington, lets players model the genetic makeup of proteins, which is a spatial cognition type of game (protein structure prediction). Through this cooperative online game, players helped researchers rapidly identify the crystal structure solution for a monkey virus related to AIDS in just a few weeks, by far outpacing researchers who had been trying to find this structure for years (Cooper et al., 2010). As I'm writing these lines in March 2020, players have just been called again for support, this time to help researchers design proteins that could fight the SARS-CoV-2 virus. In some cases, video games and gamers may truly help make the world a better place.

SOCIAL SKILLS AND SOCIAL IMPACT

In the past decades, a large body of research has focused on exploring the negative impact of video games, especially their potential to cause aggressive behavior (see Chapter 4). In contrast, very few studies have looked into their potential to foster prosocial behavior (helping others). A study by Greitemeyer and Osswald (2010) found low-cost prosocial behavior (such as helping to pick up spilled pencils) and high-cost prosocial behavior (such as helping someone who is being harassed) increased not long after playing a prosocial video game (such as Lemmings or City Crisis) for 8–10 minutes, as compared to after playing a neutral game (Tetris). Playing Lemmings (versus Tetris) was also found to promote empathy (Greitemeyer et al., 2010).

Another study has reported that playing prosocial video games (Super Mario Sunshine or Chibi Robo) was related to cooperation, sharing, empathy, and helping behavior in adolescents (Gentile et al., 2009). In a study where participants played for 30 minutes either a violent game (Quake 3, Unreal Tournament) or a non-violent game (Zuma, The Next Tetris), or they didn't play any game, those who played a non-violent game showed less aggressive behavior as measured by a task afterwards and also as compared to those who didn't play any game at all (Sestir and Bartholow, 2010). This very interesting finding suggests that participants who played no game at all generated significantly more aggressive responses post-test than non-violent game players.

Beyond these first few studies suggesting that some video games can foster prosocial behavior or reduce aggressive behavior, some video games are designed with the intention of promoting social impact or raising awareness. Just like any other media, such as movies or books, some video games intend to convey a message to its audience. For example, Papers, Please (developed by Lucas Pope) is a game where players take on the role of an immigrant officer at a fictional border and have to make moral choices about who to let through or not. PeaceMaker (developed by ImpactGames) is a government simulation game whereby players have to resolve the Israeli-Palestinian conflict peacefully. Salaam (Junub Games) is a game whereby players are in the shoes of a refugee, and which was created by Lual Mayen, who used to be a refugee himself. *Sea of Solitude* (Jo-Mei Games) aims to help players understand depression. *Eco* (Strange Loop Games) is a simulation game in which players need to collaborate to create a civilization on a planet by managing its natural resources in a sustainable way. *Sky: Children of the Light* (thatgamecompany) is a game about gifting and about meaningful social connections. *Walden, a game* (developed by Tracy Fullerton and the USC Game Innovation Lab) invites players to reflect on simple living, translating the philosophy of author Henry David Thoreau, and so on. Video game creators offer players creative and thoughtful pieces of art that can move people and make players think, just like other pieces of art can. Every year, such video games are celebrated at the Games for Change Festival, along with video games that intend to promote education or health. Video games are a rich, diverse, and interactive art form.

BENEFITS OF VIDEOGAME PLAY: TO SUM UP

Like any activity, playing video games has an impact on the brain. Among the studies conducted, the most robust ones suggest that being trained on certain commercial video games (mostly action games) can have a long-lasting positive impact on visual acuity, visual attention skills, and spatial cognition such as mental rotation. This transfer of learning on similar tasks (i.e. near transfer) is rare and thus notable. Yet, just like with music or chess (Sala and Gobet, 2017), video games are unlikely to make you "smarter"; they do not allow a transfer of the specific skills learned while playing the game to farther domains by themselves. But they can be used as a tool in a pedagogical environment. This is why educators and health practitioners are increasingly interested either in using certain existing games for education (such as *Minecraft*) or creating video games to accomplish specific education or health objectives. Although more research is needed to understand more specifically what the benefits are of playing video games, we have some leads indicating that certain games can support cognitive skills, healthy behavior, or prosocial behavior. With new adopted platforms like virtual reality, or VR, virtual embodiment is now possible and has the potential to reduce pain perception, facilitate stroke rehabilitation, or allow players to experiment within a different body (Bailey and Bailenson, 2017). And, contrary to what some people might think, video games are not smothering creativity. In fact, children who play video games score higher than those who don't on measures of creativity (Jackson et al., 2012). While it's unlikely that video games will save the world, we can still celebrate their promising potential.

All in all, it's impossible to tell whether video games are good for us. It depends largely on what video game we are talking about and the context in which it's played. There is no such thing as "effects of video games" because there are as many different types of games as there are types of books, movies, or television programs. As Bavelier and colleagues put it, "One can no more say what the effects of video games are, than one can say what the effects of food are" (Bavelier et al., 2011, p. 763). There are still many unknowns today about the specific benefits of specific games, but whenever you hear or read sensational news about video games, try to find out the details. Was it a correlational study (that cannot inform about causality) or an experimental study? How many participants were in the study, and how old were they? What specific type of game was used? What was measured specifically? Without knowing these elements, it's quite impossible to have a good understanding of what a study truly concludes. And if you're a journalist reading these lines, I would encourage you to include this information in your future reporting on video game research because the way a study was conducted is as important as its results.

4

CAN PLAYING VIDEO GAMES BE DETRIMENTAL?

There is a lot of concern around video games, just like there was with comic books, rock 'n' roll, or radio before them. New technology, practices, and art forms are usually under great scrutiny when they become popular. According to a 2019 report from the NPD Group, 73% of Americans aged 2 and older play video games. We certainly need to understand what the potential negative impact of video games is, especially on children, so that recommendations can be established. But these recommendations need to be precise and evidence based. Like I mentioned in Chapter 3, the "video games" category is not homogeneous. Moreover, the context in which children play these games is also very important to consider (motivations to play, social and economical context, etc.). Lastly, many studies researching negative impacts (just like those researching positive impacts) are correlational, which means that they cannot by themselves conclude to a causal relationship. With this in mind, let's first take a look at violence, since the majority of the research on video games has so far explored this topic.

VIDEO GAMES AND VIOLENCE

Decades of research studying the effects of violent video games on children's and teenagers' aggressive behavior have been conducted. It has been so far the main focus of the research on video games, and the least we can say is that the conclusions drawn from these studies have been heavily debated. The methodology of some studies has been put into question, and a few of them even got retracted because they turned out to be too flawed (see Ferguson, 2020 for discussion), although we will not talk about these controversial studies here. While many different types of games exist, some violent games are among the most popular ones, such as the *Call of Duty* series or *Grand Theft Auto* series. And even though these games are usually rated M for Mature (i.e. not recommended for those under 17) by the ESRB rating system, they are often played by young teenagers. It's therefore important to understand whether violent games can increase real-world aggressive behavior. By "aggressive behavior", note that experimental studies are mostly looking into mild behaviors, such as putting hot sauce in someone's sandwich if they don't like spicy food. So this is "prank level" aggression, not pushing, shouting, or fighting.

Much of the research on violent video games has been guided by a theoretical framework called "General Aggression Model" (GAM), which is a model designed to account for aggressive behavior in general. Regarding our subject matter, it suggests that violent game play increases aggressive thoughts, feelings, and behavior in the short term, as well as aggressive attitudes and aggression desensitization in the long term (Anderson et al., 2007). GAM is inspired by professor of psychology Albert Bandura's social learning theory. This theory, later renamed "social cognitive theory", posits that humans learn not only by direct manipulation of the environment but also by observing others. Thus, we can learn new behaviors and form new beliefs based on what we see others do, and this includes aggressive behaviors (Bandura, 1978). Aggression here is defined as a behavior intended to harm someone else or to cause physical destruction. However, it is important to note that Bandura's studies of aggression have been criticized as not, in fact, telling us much about aggression at all (Tedeschi and Quigley, 1996). In summary, according to Bandura, role models can influence people's behavior, in good and bad.

But could a virtual interactive environment have the same effect? The GAM is now being referred as the "General Learning Model" (GLM), which posits that any stimulus (including video games) is expected to have short-term and long-term effects through several learning mechanisms. Thus, depending on the content of the game, the GLM predicts that its impact will be different. Per this theory, prosocial video games should increase both short-term and long-term prosocial behavior, while violent video games should increase short-term and long-term aggressive behavior. In the previous chapter, we talked about a study showing that some prosocial video games can foster prosocial behavior (Greitemeyer and Osswald, 2010). Similarly, some scholars worry that violent games can foster aggressive behavior, such as players administering noise blasts to someone after playing a violent game, although other scholars do not find this outcome in their research. The question is then to understand if this impact, if confirmed, is lingering and if it's meaningful; in short, the burning question is mainly to find out whether playing violent video games can influence individuals to commit violent acts in real life.

Anderson and colleagues (2010) conducted a meta-analysis of numerous correlational, experimental, and longitudinal studies in an effort to draw solid conclusions (a longitudinal study spans across several weeks, months, or even years). Their analysis revealed that violent video game exposure was positively associated with aggressive behavior and feelings, desensitization against violent content, lack of empathy, and lack of prosocial behavior. However, as we have mentioned before, a correlation does not inform on causality, and other researchers have pointed out that it's possible, for example, that individuals who have aggressive behavior and feelings could be more attracted to playing violent video games. This is why Anderson and colleagues looked into longitudinal studies, and their analysis suggested that playing violent video games is a causal risk factor for long-term harmful outcomes, such as aggressive behavior and desensitization. Lastly, the authors of this meta-analysis pointed out that experimental studies showed short-term effects of violent video games on aggression, although they acknowledged that these effects seem to be largely the result of what we call "priming" (i.e. the expo-sure to some stimulus temporarily activates a related thought, like the exposure of the word "chair" may temporarily activate the thought of a table). The authors concluded that violent videogame play was a causal risk factor for aggressive behavior. However, using the same dataset of studies as Anderson and colleagues (2010), Hilgard and colleagues (2017) performed a re-analysis and concluded that the experimental evidence for the violent video game effects are less sound than how Anderson and colleagues presented it. Hilgard and colleagues thus suggested that theories of aggression may be weaker than previously thought and emphasized the nature of "priming" in the effects observed: merely thinking about a behavior (such as aggressive feelings when playing a violent video game) increases the likelihood of performing that behavior in the short term.

The GAM has come under significant criticism, and some studies also explicitly have not found evidence to support the GAM. For example, a recent study by Przybylski and Weinstein (2019) inves-tigated whether teenagers (over one thousand participants aged 14 and 15 years) who spend time playing violent video games exhibit higher levels of aggressive behavior when compared with those who do not. Their results did not find violent video game engagement to be associated with observable variability in adolescents' aggres-sive behavior. Another recent study by Kühn (2019) explored this topic in a longitudinal study, this time by exposing adult partic-ipants to two different types of video games for a period of two months and investigating this impact on several measures assessing aggression, impulsivity-related constructs, mood, anxiety, empa-thy, interpersonal competencies, and executive control functions. One group of participants played the violent game *Grand Theft Auto V* (Rockstar Games) for two months while a control group played the non-violent life simulation game *The Sims* 3 (published by Elec-tronic Arts), and another control group was not playing any game. Participants were tested before and after the long-term intervention (i.e. playing the game for two months) and at a follow-up appoint-ment two months later. The results did not reveal relevant negative effects in response to playing the violent video game, therefore suggesting that the GAM was not supported. Other theories suggest that media is too distal and weak to have much effect on aggressive behavior. For example, the "catalyst model" theory suggests instead that aggression and violent behavior are caused by genetic predispositions coupled with harsh early environments and current stress (Ferguson et al., 2008).

There are thus seemingly two camps in game research on this topic: one that argues that violent video games increase aggression durably in its players, and the other one that disagrees. In an effort to clarify this matter, the American Psychological Association (APA) selected experts who were not supposed to be primary stakeholders in any of the "camps" to examine the literature. The goal was to update APA's knowledge and policy about the impact of violent videogame play. In their review, these experts (Calvert et al., 2017) found that violent video game exposure was associated with an increased aggressive behavior and feeling, an increased desensitization, and a decreased empathy. They concluded that "violent video game use is a risk factor for adverse outcomes, but found insufficient studies to examine any potential link between violent video game use and delinquency or criminal behavior". In short, playing violent video games was not found to cause their players to commit acts of violence in real life. In February 2020, the APA published an updated resolution saying that real life violence, such as mass shootings, should not be attributed to violent video game use based on the current available body of research. You can read this resolution here: www.apa.org/about/policy/resolution-violent-video-games.pdf. This too, attracted controversy as the APA's own media psychology division released an open letter[1] to the APA stating that their conclusions about games being linked to aggressive behavior were misleading, given inconsistent evidence in the field. As such, the APA and its own media psychology division are at odds on this matter.

Although violent video games are unlikely to cause real life violence, some gamers can trash-talk or commit antisocial behaviors such as bullying while playing an online game, and we will tackle these elements further down. It was also suggested that racing video games could increase players' risk-taking inclinations (Fischer et al., 2009). However, at present, the evidence for aggression effects caused by video gaming remains mixed. Although the debate regarding aggressive impacts is still raging, if you have children or teenagers playing video games, it is recommended to check the content rating of these games on the ESRB.org (in North America) or PEGI.info (in Europe) websites, created specifically to help parents make informed decisions. Additionally, it seems that negative effects of violent video games can be lessened when players play them cooperatively in a team. When players work together as teammates and assist each other to accomplish a common objective, it reduces the negative effects of violent videogame play (i.e. enhances cooperation with a partner after playing the game) as compared to playing solo. Cooperative team play was found to promote feelings of cohesion, which activated trust norms, which in turn increased cooperative behavior (Greitemeyer et al., 2012).

SCHOOL PERFORMANCE

We saw in the previous chapter that playing video games can enhance visual attention skills. However, there are concerns that fast-paced video games could negatively impact the ability of players (especially children) to remain focused on a task and exercise cognitive control (such as when we need to filter out distraction and information that are not relevant to our current task). The main focus so far is to determine if playing video games can have a negative impact on school performance. One longitudinal study (conducted over 13 months) with more than 1,000 middle childhood participants has found an association between parent and child-reported television and video game exposure (all types of games) and teacher-reported attention problems (Swing et al., 2010). However, this study measured video game exposure globally, so it is not clear what type of games could be problematic. More importantly, correlation is not causation; it can be argued that children who have a deficit of attention are more likely drawn to play video games longer. Another correlational study has found that total television time, total video game time, and violent video game exposure are associated with teenagers' poorer grades (Gentile et al., 2004). Yet again, it could be that teenagers who do not perform well at school spend more time playing video games, whereby they can feel more competent. Moreover, other studies have not found this association (e.g. Ferguson, 2011).

In an experiment by Weis and Cerankosky (2010), families who intended to purchase a video game console were offered one for free in return for participation in the study. Sixty-four boys, aged between 6 and 9 years, participated. They were first evaluated on their reading and writing skills (pre-test). Then, half of the children received the console immediately, and half of them received it four months later. The children who received the console immediately had worse post-test performance as compared to the children who received the console later on. These results provide some experimental evidence that video games may have a negative impact on school performance. The hypothesis is that video game exposure may displace after-school activities that have educational value and may interfere with the development of reading and writing skills in some children. This is called the "displacement effect": time spent on playing a game is not spent doing other activities. For example, a correlational study found that teenage gamers spend 34% less time doing homework than non-gamers (Cummings and Vandewater, 2007).

Beyond mere video game consumption, a correlational study (Cain et al., 2016) has found that media multitasking in adolescence (e.g. playing a video game on a smartphone while watching television) was associated with poorer executive function ability (i.e. working memory capacity), worse academic achievement, and a reduced growth mindset (i.e. believing that intelligence is something we can grow). Even adults multitask (although we saw in Chapter 1 that this is not efficient) and are distracted by their smartphone. Radesky and colleagues (2014) observed caregivers with one or more young children in a fast-food restaurant and found that 72% of them used mobile devices during the meal, from the devices being placed on the table to parents' attention completely absorbed with the device rather than interacting with the child. More research is of course needed to understand the impact of video game consumption on school performance. At the very least, we can say that attempting to multitask and being distracted by our smartphones and/or video games instead of staying focused on important activities (such as homework or business work) are certainly not good for our performance.

EXCESSIVE AND PATHOLOGICAL GAMING

An increasing amount of parents are getting worried about their children becoming "addicted" to video games. Let's first try to define what an addiction is, because simply being engaged with a game and playing a lot are not enough to be considered an addiction. Note that the definition of the very nature of addiction is debated among experts (Heather, 2017), thus I'm proposing here only one simple way to define it. An addiction generally refers to a condition characterized by the compulsive use of a substance despite harmful consequences. Thus, most of the time, the term "addiction" refers to the use of a substance, such as alcohol, opioids, or tobacco; this is called "substance addiction". In these addictions, the substance generally creates a physical dependence. For example, heroin binds to opioid receptors in the brain, creating a surge of pleasurable sensation. It is extremely addictive as it disturbs the balance of hormonal and neuronal systems, and its impact cannot easily be reversed, creating a profound tolerance and physical dependence. Other substances don't create such a dramatic physical dependence, or can create a dependence that is mainly psychological, which of course does not mean that their effects are less concerning.

Other addictions are said to be "behavioral", which means that they are not substance-related, such as sex, shopping, or sports. As I'm writing these lines, only "gambling disorder" is mentioned as a behavioral addiction in the *Diagnostic and Statistical Manual of Mental Disorders* (DSM-5), the manual used by mental health professionals to diagnose mental disorders. There is also mention of an "Internet gaming disorder" in the DSM-5, but it's in the section of disorders requiring further research, along with caffeine use disorder. Nonetheless, the proposed symptoms to diagnose an Internet gaming disorder in the DSM-5, inspired by substance addiction, are as follows:

- Preoccupation with gaming;
- Withdrawal symptoms when gaming is taken away or not possible (sadness, anxiety, irritability);
- Tolerance: need to spend more time gaming to satisfy the urge;
- Inability to reduce playing, unsuccessful attempts to quit gaming;
- Giving up other activities, loss of interest in previously enjoyed activities due to gaming;
- Continuing to game despite problems;
- Deceiving family members or others about the amount of time spent on gaming;
- The use of gaming to relieve negative moods, such as guilt or hopelessness;
- Risk, having jeopardized or lost a job or relationship due to gaming.

A proposed diagnosis of Internet gaming disorder requires gaming causing "significant impairment or distress" and experiencing at least five or more of the listed symptoms within a year. Thus, experiencing any single symptom is not considered to be pathological. Having zero to four of the symptoms is considered to be within the normal range. A person's gaming habit is considered pathological when at least five of these symptoms are present and only after it has resulted in problems in several areas of their life. It is worth noting that there isn't yet a consensus on these "Internet gaming disorder" symptoms, pulled from substance addiction, and they are currently debated.

In late 2017, the World Health Organization (WHO) announced that in the upcoming edition (11th Revision) of the International Classification of Diseases (ICD), gaming disorder would be identified as a new disorder. This has resulted in some controversy. For instance, the media psychology divisions of the APA and Psychological Society of

Ireland jointly released a statement[2] disagreeing with the WHO diagnosis, claiming that the "research base is not sufficient for this disorder and that this disorder may be more a product of moral panic than good science". There is no debate that some people experience problematic or pathological gaming that might distress them and that they need help. However, the larger question heavily debated by researchers and addiction professionals alike is whether problematic gaming can or should be attributed to a new disorder (Aarseth et al., 2017). Some people have problematic behavior with sports, work, or shopping, yet there are no specific related disorders recognized by the DSM-5 or the ICD. Some researchers claim that problematic gaming should be viewed as a coping mechanism associated with underlying problems such as depression or anxiety (Plante et al., 2019). Others posit that any rewarding "operant" behavior (i.e. operant conditioning explained in Chapter 1) can become an addiction, such as consuming illicit drugs, having sex, or eating, and therefore playing video games can be "genuinely" addictive in the same way (Foddy, 2017). The latter perspective is supported by the fact that videogame play elicits the same patterns of reward activation (involving the neurochemical dopamine) as gambling, drugs, and food. Playing video games has been shown to increase the levels of dopamine in the brain by about 100% (Koepp et al., 1998), but "natural" rewards such as food or sex increase dopamine levels by 150% to 300% (Allerton and Blake, 2008). Meditation was also found to increase dopamine levels by 65% (Kjaer et al., 2002). As a comparison, an illicit drug like methamphetamine increases dopamine levels by over 1,000% (Allerton and Blake, 2008). Given these elements, binge eaters could be considered addicted to food in the same way that drug addicts are addicted to drugs. In turn, Foddy (2017) posits, "If videogames are indeed addictive, it seems reasonable to form the hypothesis that any willful behavior could be addictive".

We still don't understand the role of certain neurochemicals in addiction, such as dopamine, serotonin, or norepinephrine (Whiting et al., 2018), and it actually seems that the level of dopamine elicited by a drug (such as cocaine or alcohol) does not predict how many people will get addicted to the drug or the severity of the addiction. Reducing pathological gaming to "dopamine shots" is therefore a gross oversimplification that doesn't help us understand the nature of gaming disorder nor how to help players (and/or their close relatives) suffering from it. Additional research is clearly needed to determine the etiology and risk factors of pathological gaming, as well as the best approaches for treatment. One rather different perspective to understand pathological gaming is through self-determination theory (SDT), which we described in Chapter 1 in the motivation section. As a reminder, SDT posits that the activities satisfying the human needs for competence, autonomy, and relatedness are intrinsically motivating (as opposed to operant conditioning that is extrinsically rewarding), and therefore more engaging. Recent research has shown that gamers who are most likely to report Internet gaming disorder symptoms are those whose needs are being satisfied by gaming but not by real life (Allen and Anderson, 2018). This means that players whose intrinsic needs aren't satisfied as much in real life than they are in certain video games could be more at risk. This result is in line with another study showing that gaming disorder is a dysfunction brought on by the absence of psychological need satisfaction in the player's environment (Weinstein et al., 2017).

Researchers and addiction professionals still have a lot of work ahead of them to understand problematic gaming; its neurobiological, psychological, and social underpinnings; and whether it should have its own disorder. Nonetheless, some people have a problematic gaming behavior, which is associated with large amounts of time spent in gaming, lack of sleep, and a shortage of social contacts (Allison et al., 2006). It is important to distinguish between passionate gaming and pathological gaming, though, because doing something a lot is not enough to establish a pathological behavior. Some researchers estimated that about 0.3% to 1% of the general population might qualify for a potential diagnosis of Internet gaming disorder (Przybylski et al., 2017), while it is estimated that there are over two billion gamers across the world. Among those who play video games, it was found that more than two out of three players did not report any symptoms of Internet gaming disorder, and researchers concluded that Internet-based games might be significantly less addictive than gambling. However, in another study conducted on 1,178 American children aged 8 to 18, about 8% of videogame players were found to have pathological patterns of play. Those pathological gamers also received poorer grades in school (Gentile, 2009). It is thus necessary to conduct more research to better understand pathological gaming and establish precise recommendations for prevention and treatment to the general public and the game industry alike. In the meantime, it's also important to avoid a moral panic that could stigmatize billions of gamers while downplaying the suffering of individuals who truly suffer from pathological gaming. This is why the creation of the first gaming detox camps are raising concerns for many: in the worse-case scenario, the strong focus on videogame play could distract from the real origins of the symptoms, such as child negligence or anxiety, while many of these video game rehabilitation programs are extremely expensive. Of course, other researchers and health professionals find that now having a recognized "gaming disorder" will raise awareness on the suffering of those addicted to games and will encourage more research to ultimately help those who are suffering more adequately. In any case, if you're a parent and your children are gaming, stay vigilant regarding what type of games (and modes) they are playing and with whom, whether they are getting enough sleep and that they are not neglecting other activities (such as homework) and social contacts. Lastly, some scientists suggest that certain video games are "designed to be addictive" and compare some game mechanics to machine gambling (Schüll, 2012). We will address this topic as well as the concept of the "attention economy" in the next chapter about ethics.

In sum, pathological gaming does exist, and some people do need help. However, the scientific debate around the existence of a specific addiction to video games, and its causes and treatments, is far from a resolution. This sensitive topic requires further research, especially given the attention it gets from policy makers. In the meantime, distinguishing between passionate gaming and pathological gaming can help avoid stigmas and downplaying true addiction suffering, overall helping to foster a more constructive discourse on the topic.

SLEEP

Having enough sleep every night is essential to everyone's mental and physical health. For children and teenagers, sleep is particularly critical for a healthy development, learning, and memory. There is a growing concern that electronic media use could have a negative impact on sleep, especially among this sensitive population. Frequent use of video games has been associated (i.e. it correlates) with longer time to fall asleep (i.e. sleep onset latency), shorter total sleep time or less time in bed, and higher levels of daytime tiredness. When considering the use of computers or electronic games in the evening or at night, it has been reported that 24% of teenage Americans play video games after 9 pm. Playing video games or using a computer before bed has been associated with shorter total sleep duration, increased daytime tiredness, and poorer overall sleep quality. Thus, it appears that the use of electronic media by children and adolescents is associated with a decrease in their sleep or sleep quality in certain conditions, although the precise effects and mechanisms remain unclear (see Cain and Gradisar, 2010). However, there haven't been a lot of experimental studies conducted yet allowing us to understand the causal relationship between videogame play and sleep time and quality. Besides, the effects of videogame play on sleep found in these studies seem to be modest (Weaver et al., 2010) when participants play for about 50 minutes before going to bed. Another study compared the effect of more prolonged videogame play (150 minutes versus 50 minutes) on sleep with 17 teenage boys (King et al., 2013). The results showed that prolonged violent video gaming (150 minutes) led to a 27-minute decrease in the teenagers' total sleep time as compared with regular video gaming (50 minutes). Thus, playing violent video games for a prolonged time (150 minutes) before going to bed seems to negatively impact sleep time and is therefore not recommended.

The main concern regarding video games and sleep is three-fold: 1) time playing video games could "displace" time that could be spent sleeping instead; 2) playing action-packed violent games before going to bed could create an arousal (cognitive or physiological), increasing the time to fall asleep; and 3) bright light exposure could impact the player's circadian rhythm. This last hypothesis puts time playing video games into the bigger "screen time" bucket, which could have a negative impact on sleep. In a study analyzing data from a sample of over 50,000 American children, it was found that each hour devoted to digital screens was associated with 3 to 8 fewer minutes of sleep at night (Przybylski, 2019). Digital screen time, on its own, seems to have only a slight negative effect on sleep, so the question should rather be, What sorts of screen time activities could impact sleep? "Screen time", just like "video games" is a broad category. Many things can be done with a screen, from reading a book to chatting with a friend to watching a documentary or playing an action-packed video game. It might be more informative to look into what specific activities could negatively impact sleep. For example, regarding video games, we saw that playing a violent game for 150 minutes before going to bed has a negative impact on total sleep time, but the impact is mild when playing for 50 minutes. More research is needed to precisely define the impact of different types of games, when they are played (weekdays versus weekend days, and day play versus evening play), for how long, etc. While moderate screen time overall does not seem to negatively impact well-being (Przybylski and Weinstein, 2017), it is of course important that children, teenagers, and adults alike vary their activities throughout the day and do some physical exercise. Here again, some video games do encourage physical activity (such as the very popular game *Pokémon Go* developed by Niantic); this is why it's important to define what type of video games we are talking about when exploring health impacts. That being said, many video games are played while sitting. Although more research is again needed to understand the impact of video-game play and screen time on sleep and overall well-being, we do know that a sedentary lifestyle has a negative impact on our mental and physical health, if anything.

ANTISOCIAL BEHAVIOR

If you have ever used social media or read comments on an article online, you might have observed that people are not always communicating courteously with one another, far from it. Multiplayer online video games are not exempt from this phenomenon, especially since they are growing into full online social spaces where players can just hang out or even watch a concert. Sadly, discrimination, trash talking, bullying, or trolling are often experienced when playing online, and these behaviors are grouped into what we call "antisocial behavior", which can be felt as "toxic" by players who are victims of it. The video game industry is trying to address this problem quite seriously, as there is some evidence that experiencing antisocial behavior has a negative impact on the engagement players have with a game, not to mention that experiencing such behavior is not pleasant and can even be quite distressful. After all, the large majority of players don't opt in to be harassed when they start a game. Game studios take a number of measures to reduce antisocial behavior and protect players. The company Riot Games, for example, is well known for experimenting with ways to reduce such behavior in their multiplayer online battle arena (MOBA) game *League of Legends* (Kou and Nardi, 2013). More than 160 videogame companies have grouped into a coalition called Fair Play Alliance (fairplayalliance.org) to share best practices in the hope of efficiently reducing antisocial behavior in online games as much as possible. These efforts include establishing a code of conduct and asking players to abide by it, allowing players to report someone who is trash talking or harassing them, enforcing the code of conduct by banning confirmed violators from the game for a certain period of time, etc. There is also some evidence that if players don't feel competent (i.e. self-determination theory of intrinsic motivation), it could lead to increases in players' aggressive thoughts, feelings, and behavior (Przybylski et al., 2014), which means that games that don't allow players to feel growing mastery could be fostering antisocial behavior. While the game industry is definitely tackling this issue, antisocial behavior in online games is far from being solved, and players can be victims of it just like on any other online social platform.

Women and marginalized people are often considered to be at a greater risk of experiencing antisocial behavior online, but so are children. In their clinical report in the journal *Pediatrics*, O'Keeffe and Clarke-Pearson (2011) explain that children and teenagers are at higher risk as they navigate online because of their limited capacity for self-regulation and susceptibility to peer pressure. Issues that already existed offline (in real life), such as bullying, clique forming, and sexual experimentation, can now also be found frequently online in the shape of cyberbullying, trolling, privacy issues, and "sexting". Parents need to help their children through antisocial behavior online (and even criminal behavior such as child abuse) in the same way they need to do it in real life. The main difference is that parents are not always tech savvy, and children can potentially go online at any time, especially if they own a smartphone. It is therefore critical to educate both children and parents in media literacy, so that everyone can be safer exploring the online world.

NEGATIVE IMPACT OF VIDEOGAME PLAY: TO SUM UP

Video games, taken as a global category, are neither good nor bad. Depending on the perspective, they are considered an interactive art form, a platform, or a playful activity, and they are extremely diverse. Some video games are played mostly outdoors, others are played at home, some are violent, others are peaceful, some are played solo, and others are played competitively or cooperatively. To understand the potential detrimental effects of video games, we need to look into specifics instead of approaching "video games" as a whole. We saw in the previous chapter that the benefits of playing video games are often exaggerated, and we can make the same statement regarding their downsides. It all depends on what games are played and in what context. Violent video games seem to present the most downsides, and while some of the most popular games are violent (i.e. *Call of Duty* series, *Grand Theft Auto* series), others are not (i.e. *Minecraft*, *Pokémon* series). Also, the ESRB and PEGI rating systems can inform parents about the content of commercial games, such as violence or gambling.

Another clear downside is excessive videogame play. Even before becoming pathological, playing too much at the expense of other activities (such as homework or physical activity) and at the expense of sleeping is clearly detrimental. However, most gamers are playing moderately, including teenagers. Any activity done in excess can be detrimental, and video games follow the same rule. The challenge now would be to determine how much videogame play is too much, especially to help parents guide their young gamers, and if there are specific mechanics and situations that can encourage excessive play-time (we will address the topic of "attention economy" in the next chapter). It's also important to understand what children and teen-agers are doing when they are gaming, as video games are becoming a social platform on their own, where players can just hang out together. Social life is very important for teenagers, and a lot of social activities now happen online, including while playing video games. Today, 57% of teenagers have met a new friend online, and 52% of teens spend time with friends playing video games (Lenhart et al., 2015). It's thus important to consider this aspect when examining video game time.

As Andrew Przybylski (2014, p. 6) says, "the broad fears and hopes about gaming may be exaggerated". More precise research is needed to better understand how precisely video games impact children's well-being and behavior, and establish evidence-based guidelines, for policy makers, parents, and the video game industry alike. Playing video games, just like any other entertainment activity, should just be fun for everyone.

5

ETHICS IN THE VIDEO GAME INDUSTRY

Video games are a rich interactive art form allowing players to experience a wide variety of gameplay mechanics, worlds, concepts, and stories. They have become one of the most popular forms of entertainment in the world, and some of them are highly engaging. Video games inevitably have an impact on players, albeit overall more modest than publicized, which can be both positive and negative depending on the type of game and the context in which the game is played. The game user experience (UX) mindset that I described in Chapter 2 entails thinking about humans first, all throughout the game development process. With such an approach, game creators strive for the game to be usable, accessible, safe, and inclusive to all players, and they do their best to offer a fun and engaging experience. Principles of human factors psychology and the scientific method are thus applied to achieve this goal. We could compare this approach to magicians who use their knowledge of the brain to entertain us. For example, they manipulate our scarce attentional resources to trick us, and we agree to it because it's fun. But such manipulation of our attention can also be used by pickpockets to take advantage of us. A UX mindset entails offering a magical experience by accounting for human limitations and being respectful of players. It's certainly not about exploiting these limitations for profit. And while it's vital for a game studio and indie developers to be profitable, players' interest and well-being should always stay at the center of preoccupation, not business goals. This is why considering ethics should be a priority when establishing a game UX strategy, although it is sadly not talked about much yet in the game industry. Here I propose a few non-exhaustive elements that are important to consider when creating video games, through the lens of a UX perspective.

DARK PATTERNS

A "dark pattern" can typically happen when business goals are prioritized over humans. It refers to a design with a purposely deceiving functionality, usually aimed at maximizing a business's profit at the expense of users. It's about tricking users into doing something that can be considered a loss for them, while it is a clear win for the company behind the dark pattern. For example, imagine that you are shopping on a very popular online platform. You place a few items in your cart and are now ready to check out, so you open your cart and click on the "Proceed to checkout" button. The next screen displays a lot of text and has a big orange button at the bottom right saying "Get started". Since you're in a hurry and have other things to do, you discard the text, click on the big orange button, and then pay for your order and leave the website. Unknowingly, you've actually just subscribed to a "Prime" membership with a monthly payment, and it could take you a while to realize it (and it might even be difficult to later unsubscribe). To check out without subscribing, you needed to click on a tiny hyperlink that you didn't notice at the time because our human attention is limited. This is a clear dark pattern: the design is purposely confusing to trick people into doing something they aren't fully aware of and that is detrimental to them while beneficial for the company. Another example of a dark pattern is an advertisement displayed on your phone that consists of a picture of a pair of sneakers sold by the company sponsoring the ad, with what seems to be a hair across the screen. Users might believe it's a real hair and swipe up with their finger to get rid of it. But the hair is actually part of the advertisement, and by swiping up, users land on the company store. This again is a clear example of users being tricked to accomplish an action that benefits the company at their expense. If you're curious about dark patterns, I encourage you to visit the website darkpatterns.org by UX professional Harry Brignull.

However, dark patterns aren't always as obvious, and they can actually be quite subtle. Let's take an example described by Dan Ariely in his book *Predictably Irrational* (2008) regarding a subscription offer for a magazine. Three options were proposed:

A One-year subscription to the online version, for $59.
B One-year subscription to the print edition, for $125.
C One-year subscription to both online and print versions, for $125.

Options B and C have the same price ($125), although option C has clearly more value than B. To see how these options could impact people's choice, Ariely ran an experimental study on 100 students from MIT to see which option they would pick. Most students chose option C (84 students), 16 students chose option A, and none of them chose option B, which therefore seems a useless option; who would want to pay the same price for less value? So Ariely removed option B and ran the test again using new participants. This time, most students chose option A (68 students), while 32 students chose option C. People's behavior can be influenced by the environment, and this specific case is called the "decoy effect", whereby a distracting (decoy) option (B) makes one other more expensive option (C) seem more attractive than it would be without the presence of the decoy. We could therefore argue that the decoy effect is a dark pattern, as it clearly benefits the company (it earns more money) while it's detrimental to users (they are influenced to spend more money). The decoy effect is used by many industries and companies, and it can also be used by the game industry. In many free-to-play games, players can buy some in-game currency (such as coins or gems that can be spent in the game) with real money. A decoy is often used in sales options, which can influence players to buy a more expensive package than they would have without the decoy.

Another example of a subtle dark pattern is the use of loot boxes to monetize a game. A loot box is a reward in the shape of a card pack or a chest that players can obtain by spending in-game currency (e.g. gems). When players click to open it, they discover whether they obtained a valued item or junk. This is what we call a variable ratio reward: a reward implying chance. This type of reward was used by B.F. Skinner in his operant conditioning experiments that we described in Chapter 1. It turns out that Skinner discovered that variable rewards were surprisingly more engaging than constant and predictable rewards; the rats were pressing the lever more often when they *sometimes* obtained food from it. Random outcomes can make games more engaging and exciting in certain contexts and are, in fact, used extensively, such as any game requiring a throw of dice or a draw of cards. Using variable rewards is not a bad practice by itself. However, it starts to flirt with dark patterns when they are used to encourage people to spend more money, as is the case with slot machines . . . and loot boxes. Moreover, loot boxes are downright unethical when they are targeted to minors because the brain is immature until adulthood. One area of the brain keeps developing until about 25 years of age: the prefrontal cortex. This part of the brain, among other things, controls impulses and automatic behaviors. Children and teenagers do not have a mature prefrontal cortex, which can make automatic and conditioned responses much harder for them to control when need be. This brain immaturity explains why children are not good at self-control (they often need an adult to set limits for them) and why teenagers have a greater tendency than adults to partake in risky behaviors. Therefore, loot boxes tied to monetization are an issue when children or even teenagers play this game, especially when the game is popular and they feel particularly compelled to buy loot boxes until they obtain a prize that is fashionable. Peer pressure or even bullying, which happens in real life, say, if a teenager isn't wearing trendy brands, can happen today with virtual goods. The issue is that game developers cannot easily control who is playing their games, unlike casinos that can check customers' identification cards. This is why some countries like Belgium are banning loot boxes in games altogether, since they can be considered as gambling – at least on a psychological level – and studios cannot possibly control if underage players are going to access the game and sink time, money, or both, to get those desirable variable rewards.

These are just a few examples to illustrate what can be considered a dark pattern and why they aren't ethical to use. Sometimes what looks like a dark pattern at first glance could actually be beneficial to users and therefore be considered as a good UX practice. Let's take an example from the game *World of Warcraft* (Blizzard), a role-playing game whereby players take control of a character that they develop over time. When players want to delete their character in *World of Warcraft*, they first see a "confirmation screen" asking them to confirm their intention. But players also need to type the word "DELETE" in a text field to fully confirm. Is this a dark pattern to make people think twice before deleting a character? It's clearly not beneficial for Blizzard when players delete characters, as it could mean that they are done with the game. However, it's also beneficial for players to verify that they are not deleting their character by mistake. Players can spend hours, weeks, months, or even years developing a character, so it can thus be justified to add extra steps to avoid accidental deletions, which would result in a strong frustration. This practice is respecting the usability guideline called "error prevention" (see Chapter 2). To prevent users from taking an action that could have a negative impact for them (e.g. closing a software program after having been working for two hours in it without saving first), it is usually a good practice to increase the "physical load" (i.e. adding a click in the process) via a confirmation screen to ensure that this is really what they want to do. Asking players to type "DELETE" is ensuring that they are really paying attention to their action and are fully aware of the consequences. Therefore, this is a good UX practice. Of course, if the character had a sad face or was crying on this screen as a player is about to get rid of it, then we could argue that the emotional guilt trip would turn it into a dark pattern.

In summary, on one hand, we have dark patterns that are deceitful designs with the intention of benefiting the company at the expense of users, and on the other hand, we have good UX practices that are respectful of users even when trying to reach business goals. A third possibility is what we call "bad UX": it's a design that is confusing or allowing users to make mistakes, but it's not intentional. For example, users end up buying a product twice because it was not made clear in the interface that the first attempt was successful. This issue was overlooked in the design process rather than being intentionally deceiving. Having a UX mindset entails precisely tracking down all UX issues, especially those that can be highly detrimental to users.

Game studios that are respectful of their audience should not use dark patterns. Having a UX mindset can guide game developers and publishers in keeping players' experience at the center of their preoccupation, especially when all or part of their audience is underage players.

ATTENTION ECONOMY

Our attention is scarce and precious, and anyone who has anything to say or sell might want to grab it, sometimes using questionable techniques. Features like bottomless scrolling (such as on Facebook or Twitter), autoplay (such as on YouTube or Netflix), or push notifications (used by all social media and many mobile games) could encourage us to engage or stay engaged with a platform even if we didn't have a clear intention to do so initially. This is what we call the "attention economy". Moreover, some of these techniques are downright unethical and could be labeled as dark patterns. A compelling example of such an engagement-sustaining technique described by ethicist and ex-Googler Tristan Harris is the Snapstreak feature on Snapchat. This feature shows the number of days in a row that two Snapchat users have communicated with each other. Snapchat users are then encouraged to keep the streak growing. Tweens and teenagers are particularly vulnerable to this feature because connecting with friends is very important, no one wants to be the jerk who breaks a 150-day streak, and because the brain is immature until adulthood.

Here again, it's not always easy to determine when a feature is a good UX practice and when it starts sliding into the dark side. For example, loyalty programs are generally accepted and even expected; when we are loyal to a store, a brand, or a game, we might expect some commercial gesture rewarding our loyalty. If every morning you buy your coffee at the same local coffee shop, you might appreciate receiving a free coffee every now and then. You might also appreciate a loyalty program that offers you, say, a mug after 30 coffees consumed. Now, imagine a slightly different scenario: the coffee shop starts a promotional campaign, and customers can receive a collector mug autographed by a famous artist. To earn it, you need to buy 30 coffees before the end of the campaign, which lasts only one month (30 days). After that, the mug will never be offered again. As you can see, this scenario goes beyond rewarding customers' loyalty. If people really want the mug, they will have to drink one coffee per day at this shop, even if they didn't feel like it. More than rewarding engagement with a product, this is punishing disengagement, because if you skip drinking coffee one day, you will never get the reward.

Free-to-play games need players to retain (i.e. come back regularly) in the hope that they will buy something one day so that the studio can stay afloat. Therefore rewarding loyalty, in the form of giving a reward when players come back, is often used. The ethical line is crossed when games punish disengagement – for example, by requiring players to log in a certain number of cumulative days to reach a highly desired reward, or a game with seasonal rewards influencing players to engage with the game very regularly if they want a chance to earn enough points every time they play to afford the reward before it's forever gone, thus capitalizing on the "fear of missing out", or FOMO.

When companies place their business and revenues first without considering all users' well-being, then they are leaning more towards dark pattern practices. Companies that think about users first, in a win-win mindset (beneficial to both users and the business), are leaning towards a UX strategy and culture. The game industry needs to think about ethics and define what lines should not be crossed.

Making games is a hard endeavor; most free-to-play games are barely surviving while gamers are increasingly demanding. If the game doesn't provide new content at a regular pace, players get bored and move on to another game, which could mean the end of the project or even the studio (see, for example, the demise of Telltale, the studio behind *The Walking Dead* video game series). As a result, many studios often copy a business model (e.g. seasons) or feature (e.g. loot boxes) that seemed to work well in a certain game to keep their own game afloat, without asking themselves if it's ethical or not. And some studios might be fully aware of the impact of these mechanics and be using them on purpose. Game developers need to have a better understanding of the psychological impact of certain engaging techniques they use, especially if their games are played by children and teenagers. The game industry could encourage a healthier gaming behavior by *rewarding* disengagement, such as the rest system in *World of Warcraft*, allowing players who took a break to gain additional experience points when they resume playing. At the very least, punishing disengagement should always be avoided.

GAME CONTENT

We saw in Chapter 4 that violent video games are not causing players to commit violent acts in real life. But it's not a reason for game developers not to pay attention to the content of their games. No design is ever neutral. A game inevitably encourages some behaviors (i.e. rewards, or doesn't punish), while it discourages other behaviors (punishes, or doesn't reward). Game developers use this knowledge to help players navigate the game and overall have fun. However, some behaviors that aren't desired or by design, such as antisocial behaviors, can sometimes happen in games when they were not anticipated or controlled for. Many multiplayer games have codes of conduct and might punish players who behave in a harmful way against other players (e.g. harassing them) by banning them for a certain amount of time, for example.

At the very least, game studios should monitor what behaviors they are encouraging and discouraging in their games to ensure that all players can have fun while being safe within the game and on their community management platforms. Moreover, game developers need to reflect on what they are normalizing (or worse, glorifying) in the name of fun. As Miguel Sicart puts it in his book *The Ethics of Computer Games* (2009. p. 22), "Games force behaviors by rules". My point here is not within a virtue ethics perspective that would define playing games with immoral actions content (such as killing virtual people) as being an unethical activity. Rather, my contention is aligned with Sicart in considering the player as a moral agent who can make choices within the game environment. For example, players can choose to drive over and kill pedestrians in *Grand Theft Auto V*, while this is not a choice that players of *Driver: San Francisco* have (pedestrians in the latter game always end up avoiding cars). So-called sandbox games surely offer players more agency than scripted games, yet players' agency is still limited by what was planned by game designers. For example, players in *GTA: Vice City* (rated Mature on the ESRB system and 18+ on the PEGI system) can choose to have sex with a prostitute to gain extra health and can decide to kill the prostitute afterwards to regain their money. Within the system of the game and given its virtual aspect, this action is not necessarily immoral, and gamers will argue that this is a good way to maximize in-game benefits while it minimizes in-game costs (behavior usually called "min-maxing"). However, the game does not offer another way to min-max health in the prostitute example. The game system doesn't allow players to make friends or fall in love with the prostitute, which could in turn diminish the cost of getting increased health. Therefore the "sandbox" aspect of the game is still limited by what behaviors are allowed, rewarded, and punished by game designers. When unethical actions are rewarded in a game while their moral opposites are not even a possibility (for example, both ethical and unethical actions are possible in the game *Black & White* developed by Lionhead Studios), we can argue that these games have unethical content.

Arguing that some games have unethical content is not the same as saying that these games have a real-life immoral impact on society. Yet it's not a reason not to reflect on the ethics of game content. Besides, there is some evidence, albeit still uncertain, that screen media could have an impact on players' attitudes, beliefs, and prejudices toward certain populations. For example, how the media portrays women and various marginalized groups could be influencing stereotypes and behavior towards such groups. Saleem and Anderson (2013) found that brief play of a common stereotypical violent game in which Muslim characters are portrayed as enemy terrorists increased stereotyping against this population. Another study (Saleem et al., 2017) showed that exposure to news stories portraying Muslims as terrorists is positively associated with Americans' support of public policies that harm Muslims domestically and internationally.

Our cognition (i.e. knowledge) has an impact on our perception, and the culture we grow up in likely shapes our stereotypes towards certain populations, especially when these stereotypes are not clearly condemned in a society, although we do not currently understand this impact well. If you consistently witness women portrayed as being less competent than men in the entertainment industry, and that this stereotype is not strongly condemned in your environment, you might implicitly integrate this harmful stereotype as being generally true. Similarly, if you constantly see in advertisements and movies that toothpaste is spread on the entire length of the toothbrush, you might integrate that this is the expected and correct behavior to have (it's not; using a pea-sized amount of toothpaste is what is actually recommended). Of course, how we are supposed to behave with women and marginalized populations is nowhere near comparable to our behavior with toothpaste. My point is that we are constantly conditioned, influenced, and manipulated by our environment and culture, sometimes in good ways, sometimes in harmful ways. And video games today represent a big market share in our entertainment consumption. Although any given game doesn't by itself have an impact on, say, how women perceive their body (Lindner et al., 2019), it is hard to argue against the fact that women are objectified overall in our culture, which in turn has inevitably some sort of impact on the implicit biases reinforced in the population. While it's not the fault of the game industry if such stereotypes and prejudice exist, they are now part of our culture and therefore the game industry has some level of responsibility to consider.

ETHICS IN THE GAME INDUSTRY: TO SUM UP

Video games are increasingly influential in our society. They are an art form and now part of our culture. As such, ethical considerations should be a higher priority in the game industry. Striving to offer the best experience possible to players also entails identifying and avoiding dark patterns, not falling into the so-called attention economy, and paying attention to the moral values conveyed by the game. The subject of ethics is a delicate topic, and things are rarely black or white. Establishing a code of ethics in game studios could help developers and publishers navigate the shades of grey, define the lines that cannot be crossed, and ensure that players can have fun while always being respected.

CONCLUSION

Playing a game is an experience that happens in our mind. This is why understanding the brain's capabilities and limitations can greatly help game creators accomplish their goals. Creating games is hard, and thousands of games are released every year, making it difficult for game studios and indie developers to stand out. Game user experience (UX) is the mindset that can guide them throughout the development process by always keeping the target audience at the center of their preoccupation and decisions. Game UX takes its roots in cognitive science – including psychology, applies principles of human-computer interaction, and uses the scientific method to ensure that the game team is staying on track with the experience they want to offer to their audience. To simplify, we can say that it's the psychology and overall science behind making good games. The two main pillars of a game UX framework are usability (i.e. the ability of the game to be easy to discover and interact with) and engage-ability (i.e. the ability of the game to be engaging). As each game is different, this framework provides guidelines, or ingredients for crafting fun, with the hopes of delighting all players.

Once the game is released and finally experienced by players, it will have an impact on them, just like anything humans experience in life. But as games are interactive and sometimes highly engaging, they have the potential to be more influential. This is why scholars investigate the psychology and overall science of playing games. Many claims are made about the benefits and potential detriments of video games, and in general those claims are exaggerated and often based on opinion. The evidence suggests that certain games can have cognitive benefits, especially with regard to visual attention skills and spatial cognition, but they won't likely make you overall "smarter". In some cases, commercial video games can be used effectively for educational and health benefits, but oftentimes the benefits actually stem from a passionate educator or a supportive health professional moderating gameplay rather than from the game itself. In this sense, video games can be used as a tool for good, and we need to understand this potential better. They are also a cultural platform for raising awareness and encouraging social impact in our society. However, certain video games can have downsides, too. Violent games might foster mild aggressive feelings and behaviors (although this claim is heavily debated among scholars), and some players can suffer from pathological gaming. In some studies, playing certain video games past a certain amount of time was associated with poorer school performance and sleep. Lastly, online multiplayer games can expose players to antisocial behavior, which is not a good experience and is tackled seriously but more or less successfully by game studios.

For a large majority of gamers, who number over two billion across the world today, playing video games is simply a fun activity. As a category, video games are not homogeneous; there are as many types of video games as there are flavors in food. In this sense, video games are not going to save the world, nor are they forces of evil. Yet their strengths and limitations must be accounted for, and important discussions around game ethics are needed. Having a UX mindset means respecting players and always considering their well-being. A game UX perspective is about offering the best experience possible to all players, which entails consideration of accessibility, inclusion, and protection against antisocial behavior. Other ethical considerations are important to account for, especially regarding the game business model (i.e. avoiding dark patterns and attention economy tricks) and the content offered.

When these limitations are accounted for, video games represent an exciting medium that provides infinite ways to experiment with different environments, concepts, and emotions. I'm enthusiastically looking forward to discovering how their power will be creatively used in the future for education, health, and social impact, or just for creating new ways of having fun. Because they allow players to experiment and learn by doing while offering them immediate feedback, video games represent an incomparable medium that I hope will be successfully exploited in the future.

In the wake of tragedies happening in our world, such as a pandemic, systemic racism and injustice, a massive worldwide refugee crisis, and the climate emergency, we can often feel helpless. Video games can let us experiment with systems and observe our individual and collective impact on the world in playful simulations, such as the game *Plague Inc.* (Ndemic Creations) and *Eco* (Strange Loop). Progress in technology, such as artificial intelligence or the rise of new platforms (e.g. virtual reality or augmented reality), will certainly enrich our game play in ways we cannot yet fathom. We need better public understanding of games: how they are made, why they are loved, and what the culture is around them. We also need more research exploring their potential, and a more balanced discourse whether it comes from the public, policy makers, scholars, or journalists reporting on research findings. Having a precise and evidence-based understanding of the potential benefits and limitations of video games will allow us to exploit this exciting medium in the best way possible. It will also allow us to better understand when and why video games are not the best medium to accomplish certain educational, health, or social impact goals. Video games do show great potential in certain situations. There is no reason why we shouldn't explore this potential and nurture it for the greater good.

Most video games are made by passionate designers, artists, engineers, and many others who want to suspend players' disbelief and offer them a positive and magical experience. They are a rich and diverse art form and a part of our culture. I hope that this book has reinforced your love for video games if you're a gamer or made you want to become one if you're not. Thank you for allowing me to take you on this journey, and, as gamers say, "GLHF": good luck, have fun!

FURTHER READING

D. Bavelier and R. J. Davidson (2003). Brain training: games to do you good. *Nature*, 494, 425–426: www.nature.com/articles/494425a

Blumberg, F.C., Brooks, P.J. (Eds.) (2017). *Cognitive Development in Digital Contexts*. London: Academic Press.

C. Hodent (2017). *The Gamer's Brain: How Neuroscience and UX Can Impact Video Game Design*. Boca Raton: CRC Press.

C. Jarrett (2014). *Great Myths of the Brain*. New York: John Wiley & Sons.

A. Jordan and D. Romer (Eds.) (2014). *Media and the Well-Being of Children and Adolescents*. New York: Oxford University Press.

R.T. Kellogg (2007). *Fundamentals of Cognitive Psychology*. Los Angeles: SAGE Publications.

D. A. Norman (2013). *The Design of Everyday Things, Revised and Expanded Edition*. New York: Basic Books.

M. Sicart. (2009). *The Ethics of Computer Games*. Cambridge: MIT Press.

T. Stafford and M. Webb (2005). *Mind Hacks: Tips & Tools for Using your Brain*. Sebastapol, CA: O'Reilly.

NOTES

INTRODUCTION

1 www.businessinsider.com/minecraft-monthly-player-number-microsoft-2019-9?
2 www.theverge.com/2018/10/4/17934166/telltale-games-studio-closed-lay offs-end-the-walking-dead

CHAPTER 3

1 https://whimc.education.illinois.edu

CHAPTER 4

1 www.scribd.com/document/448927394/Division-46-Letter-to-the-APA-criticizing-it-s-recent-review-of-video-game-violence-literature#download
2 You can read this statement here: https://div46amplifier.com/2018/06/21/an-official-division-46-statement-on-the-who-proposal-to-include-gaming-related-disorders-in-icd-11/

REFERENCES

Aarseth, E., Bean, A. M., Boonen, H., Colder Carras, M., Coulson, M., Das, D., Deleuze, J., Dunkels, E., Edman, J., Ferguson, C. J., Haagsma, M. C., Helmersson Bergmark, K., Hussain, Z., Jansz, J., Kardefelt-Winther, D., Kutner, L., Markey, P., Nielsen, R. K., Prause, N., Przybylski, A., Quandt, T., Schimmenti, A., Starcevic, V., Stutman, G., Van Looy, J., & Van Rooij, A. J. (2017). Scholars' open debate paper on the World Health Organization ICD-11 gaming disorder proposal. *Journal of Behavioral Addiction, 6,* 267–270.

Allen, J. J., & Anderson, C. A. (2018). Satisfaction and frustration of basic psychological needs in the real world and in video games predict Internet gaming disorder scores and well-being. *Computers in Human Behavior, 84,* 220–229.

Allerton, M., & Blake, W. (2008). The "Party Drug" crystal methamphetamine: Risk factor for the acquisition of HIV. *The Permanente Journal, 12,* 56–58.

Allison, S. E., von Wahlde, L., Shockley, T., & Gabbard, G. O. (2006). The development of the self in the era of the internet and role-playing fantasy games. *American Journal of Psychiatry, 163,* 381–385.

Anderson, C. A., Gentile, D. A., & Buckley, K. E. (2007). *Violent Video Game Effects on Children and Adolescents: Theory, Research, and Public Policy.* New York: Oxford University Press.

Anderson, C. A., Shibuya, A., Ihori, N., Swing, E. L., Bushman, B. J., Sakamoto, A., Rothstein, H. R., & Saleem, M. (2010). Violent video game effects on aggression, empathy, and prosocial behavior in Eastern and Western countries. *Psychological Bulletin, 136,* 151–173.

Anguera, J. A., Boccanfuso, J., Rintoul, J. L., Al-Hashimi, O., Faraji, F., Janowich, J., Kong, E., Larraburo, Y., Rolle, C., Johnston, E., & Gazzaley, A. (2013). Video game training enhances cognitive control in older adults. *Nature, 501,* 97–101.

Ariely, D. (2008). *Predictably Irrational: The Hidden Forces That Shape Our Decisions.* New York: Harper Collins.

Bailey, J. O., & Bailenson, J. N. (2017). Immersive virtual reality and the developing child. In F. Blumberg & P. Brooks (Eds.), *Cognitive Development in Digital Contexts* (pp. 181–200). Amsterdam, Netherlands: Elsevier.

Bandura, A. (1978). Social learning theory of aggression. *Journal of Communication, 28,* 12–29.

Baranowski, T., Buday, R., Thompson, D. I., & Baranowski, J. (2008). Playing for real: Video games and stories for health-related behavior change. *American Journal of Preventive Medicine, 34,* 74–82.

Bavelier, D., Green, C. S., Han, D. H., Renshaw, P. F., Merzenich, M. M., & Gentile, D. A. (2011). Brains on video games. *Nature Reviews Neuroscience, 12,* 763–768. Retrieved from www.ncbi.nlm.nih.gov/pmc/articles/PMC4633025/

Cain, M. S., Leonard, J. A., Gabrieli, J. D. E., & Finn, A. S. (2016). Media multitasking in adolescence. *Psychonomic Bulletin & Review, 23,* 1932–1941.

Cain, N., & Gradisar, M. (2010). Electronic media use and sleep in school-aged children and adolescents. *Sleep Medicine, 11,* 735–742.

Calvert, S. L., Appelbaum, M., Dodge, K. A., Graham, S., Nagayama Hall, G. C., Hamby, S., Fasig-Caldwell, L. G., Citkowicz, M., Galloway, D. P., & Hedges, L. V. (2017). The american psychological association task force assessment of violent video games: Science in the service of public interest. *The American Psychologist, 72,* 126–143.

Cooper, S., Khatib, F., Treuille, A., Barbero, J., Lee, J., Beenen, M., & Popovic, Z. (2010). Predicting protein structures with a multiplayer online game. *Nature, 466,* 756–760.

Csikszentmihalyi, M. (1990). *Flow: The Psychology of Optimal Experience.* New York: Harper Perennial.

Cummings, H. M., & Vandewater, E. A. (2007). Relation of adolescent video game play to time spent in other activities. *Archives of Pediatrics & Adolescent Medicine, 161,* 684–689.

Dewey, J. (1913). *Interest and Effort in Education.* Cambridge: Houghton Mifflin.

Dweck, C. (2006). *Mindset: The New Psychology of Success.* New York: Random House.

Dye, M. W. G., & Bavelier, D. (2010). Differential development of visual attention skills in school-age children. *Vision Research*, 50, 452–459.

Ebbinghaus, H. (1885). *Über das Gedächtnis*. Leipzig: Dunker. Translated Ebbinghaus, H. (1913/1885). *Memory: A Contribution To Experimental Psychology* (H. A. Ruger & C. E. Bussenius, Trans.). New York: Teachers College, Columbia University.

Ferguson, C. J. (2011). The influence of television and video game use on attention and school problems: A multivariate analysis with other risk factors controlled. *Journal of Psychiatric Research*, 45, 808–813.

Ferguson, C. J. (2020). Aggressive video games research emerges from its replication crisis (Sort of). *Current Opinion in Psychology*, 36, 1–6.

Ferguson, C. J., Rueda, S., Cruz, A., Ferguson, D., Fritz, S., & Smith, S. M. (2008). Violent video games and aggression: Causal relationship or byproduct of family violence and intrinsic violence motivation? *Criminal Justice and Behavior*, 35, 311–332.

Fischer, P., Greitemeyer, T., Morton, T., Kastenmüller, A., Postmes, T., Frey, D., Kubitzki, J., & Odenwälder, J. (2009). The racing-game effect: Why do video racing games increase risk-taking inclinations? *Personality and Social Psychology Bulletin*, 35, 1395–1409.

Foddy, B. (2017). The pleasures and perils of operant behavior. In N. Heather & G. Segal (Eds.), *Addiction and Choice: Rethinking the Relationship* (pp. 49–65). Oxford, UK: Oxford University Press.

Franceschini, S., Gori, S., Ruffino, M., Viola, S., Molteni, M., & Facoetti, A. (2013). Action video games make dyslexic children read better. *Current Biology*, 23, 462–466.

Gentile, D. A. (2009). Pathological video-game use among youth ages 8–18: A national study. *Psychological Science*, 20, 594–602.

Gentile, D. A., Anderson, C. A., Yukawa, S., Ihori, N., Saleem, M., Ming, L. K., Shibuya, A., Liau, A. K., Khoo, A., Bushman, B. J., Huesmann, L. R., & Sakamoto, A. (2009). The effects of prosocial video games on prosocial behaviors: International evidence from correlational, longitudinal, and experimental studies. *Personality and Social Psychology Bulletin*, 35, 752–763.

Gentile, D. A., Lynch, P. J., Linder, J. R., & Walsh, D. A. (2004). The effects of violent video game habits on adolescent hostility, aggressive behaviors, and school performance. *Journal of Adolescence*, 27, 5–22.

Green, C. S., & Bavelier, D. (2003). Action video game modifies visual selective attention. *Nature, 423*, 534–537.

Greitemeyer, T., Agthe, M., Turner, R., & Gschwendtner, C. (2012). Acting prosocially reduces retaliation: Effects of prosocial video games on aggressive behavior. *European Journal of Social Psychology, 42*, 235–242.

Greitemeyer, T., & Osswald, S. (2010). Effects of prosocial video games on prosocial behavior. *Journal of Personality and Social Psychology, 98*, 211–221.

Greitemeyer, T., Osswald, S., & Brauer, M. (2010). Playing prosocial video games increases empathy and decreases schadenfreude. *Emotion, 10*, 796–802.

Guernsey, L., & Levine, M. (2015). *Tap, Click, Read: Growing Readers in a World of Screens.* San Francisco: Jossey-Bass.

Heather, N. (2017). On defining addiction. In N. Heather & G. Segal (Eds.), *Addiction and Choice: Rethinking the Relationship.* Oxford: Oxford University Press.

Hilgard, J., Engelhardt, C. R., & Rouder, J. N. (2017). Overstated evidence for short-term effects of violent games on affect and behavior: A reanalysis of Anderson et al. 2010. *Psychological Bulletin, 143*, 757–774.

Hirsh-Pasek, K., Golinkoff, R., Berk, L., & Singer, D. (2009). *A Mandate for Playful Learning in Preschool: Presenting the Evidence.* New York: Oxford University Press.

Hodent, C. (2017). *The Gamer's Brain: How Neuroscience and UX Can Impact Video Game Design.* Boca Raton: CRC Press.

Jackson, L. A., Witt, E. A., Games, A. I., Fitzgerald, H. E., von Eye, A., & Zhao, Y. (2012). Information technology use and creativity: Findings from the children and technology project. *Computers in Human Behavior, 28*, 370–376.

Jaeggi, S. M., Buschkuehl, M., Jonides, J., & Shah, P. (2011). Short and long-term benefits of cognitive training. *Proceedings of the National Academy of Sciences of the United States of America, 108*, 10081–10086.

Kahneman, D. (2011). *Thinking, Fast and Slow.* New York: Farrar, Straus and Giroux.

Kato, P. M., Cole, S. W., Bradlyn, A. S., & Pollock, B. H. (2008). A video game improves behavioral outcomes in adolescents and young adults with cancer: A randomized trial. *Pediatrics, 122*, e305–e317.

King, D. L., Gradisar, M., Drummond, A., Lovato, N., Wessel, J., Micic, G., Douglas, P., & Delfabbro, P. (2013). The impact of prolonged violent video-gaming on adolescent sleep: An experimental study. *Journal of Sleep Research, 22*, 137–143.

Kjaer, T.W., Bertelsen, C., Piccini, P., Brooks, D., Alving, J., & Lou, H. C. (2002). Increased dopamine tone during meditation-induced change of consciousness. *Cognitive Brain Research, 13*, 255–259.

Klahr, D., & Carver, S. M. (1988). Cognitive objectives in a LOGO debugging curriculum: Instruction, learning, and transfer. *Cognitive Psychology*, *20*, 362–404.

Koepp, M. J., Gunn, R. N., Lawrence, A. D., Cunningham, V. J., Dagher, A., Jones, T., Brooks, D. J., Bench, C. J., & Grasby, P. M. (1998). Evidence for striatal dopamine release during a video game. *Nature*, *393*, 266–268.

Kou, Y., & Nardi, B. (2013). Regulating anti-social behavior on the internet: The example of league of legends. In Proceedings of the 2013 iConference iSchools.

Kowert, R. (2019). *Video Games and Well-being: Press Start*. New York: Palgrave.

Kühn, S., Kugler, D., Schmalen, K., Weichenberger, M., Witt, C., & Gallinat, J. (2019). Does playing violent video games cause aggression? A longitudinal intervention study. *Molecular Psychiatry*, *24*, 1220–1234.

Lane, H. C., & Yi, S. (2017). Playing with virtual blocks: Minecraft as a learning environment for practice and research. In F. C. Blumberg & P. J. Brooks (Eds.), *Cognitive Development in Digital Contexts* (pp. 145–166). New York: Academic Press.

Lenhart, A., Smith, A., Anderson, M., Duggan, M., & Perrin, A. (2015). *Teens, Technology and Friendships*. Retrieved from www.pewresearch.org/wp-content/ uploads/sites/9/2015/08/Teens-and-Friendships-FINAL2.pdf

Li, R. J., Polat, U., Makous, W., & Bavelier, D. (2009). Enhancing the contrast sensitivity function through action video game training. *Nature Neuroscience*, *12*, 549–551.

Li, R. W., Ngo, C., Nguyen, J., & Levi, D. M. (2011). Video-game play induces plasticity in the visual system of adults with amblyopia. *PLoS Biology*, *9*(8), e1001135.

Lieberman, D. (2001). Management of chronic pediatric diseases with interactive health games: Theory and research findings. *Journal of Ambulatory Care Management*, *24*, 26–38.

Lindner, D., Trible, M., Pilato, I., & Ferguson, C. J. (2019). Examining the effects of exposure to a sexualized female video game protagonist on women's body image. *Psychology of Popular Media Culture*. Advance online publication.

Loftus, E. F., & Palmer, J. C. (1974). Reconstruction of automobile destruction: An example of the interaction between language and memory. *Journal of Verbal Learning and Verbal Behavior*, *13*, 585–589.

McGonigal, J. (2011). *Reality Is Broken: Why Games Make Us Better and How They Can Change the World*. New York: Penguin Press.

Norman, D. A. (2005). *Emotional Design: Why We Love (or Hate) Everyday Things*. New York: Basic Books.

Norman, D. A. (2013). *The Design of Everyday Things*. Revised and Expanded Edition. New York: Basic Books.

Okagaki, L., & Frensch, P. A. (1994). Effects of video game playing on measures of spatial performance: Gender effects in late adolescence. *Journal of Applied Developmental Psychology*. Special Issue: Effects of interactive entertainment technologies on development, 15, 33–58.

O'Keeffe, G. S., & Clarke-Pearson, K. (2011). The impact of social media on children, adolescents, and families. *Pediatrics*, 127, 800–804.

Papastergiou, M. (2009). Exploring the potential of computer and video games for health and physical education: A literature review. *Computers & Education*, 53, 603–622.

Papert, S. (1980). *Mindstorms. Children, Computers, and Powerful Ideas*. New York: Basic Books.

Piaget, J. (1962). *Play, Dreams and Imitation in Childhood* (Vol. 24). New York: Norton.

Plante, C. N., Gentile, D. A., Groves, C. L., Modlin, A., & Blanco-Herrera, J. (2019). Video games as coping mechanisms in the etiology of video game addiction. *Psychology of Popular Media Culture*, 8, 385–394.

Przybylski, A. K. (2014). Electronic gaming and psychosocial adjustment. *Pediatrics*, 134(3), e716–e722.

Przybylski, A. K. (2019). Digital screen time and pediatric sleep: Evidence from a preregistered cohort study. *The Journal of Pediatrics*, 205, 218–223.

Przybylski, A. K., Deci, E. L., Rigby, C., & Ryan, R. M. (2014). Competence-impeding electronic games and players' aggressive feelings, thoughts, and behaviors. *Journal of Personality and Social Psychology*, 106, 441–457.

Przybylski, A. K., & Weinstein, N. (2017). A large-scale test of the Goldilocks hypothesis. *Psychological Science*, 28, 204–215.

Przybylski, A. K., & Weinstein, N. (2019). Violent video game engagement is not associated with adolescents' aggressive behaviour: Evidence from a registered report. *Royal Society Open Science*, 6, 171474.

Przybylski, A. K., Weinstein, N., & Murayama, K. (2017). Internet gaming disorder: Investigating the clinical relevance of a new phenomenon. *American Journal of Psychiatry*, 174, 230–236.

Radesky, J. S., Kistin, C. J., Zuckerman, B., Nitzberg, K., Gross, J., Kaplan-Sanoff, M., & Silverstein, M. (2014). Patterns of mobile device use by caregivers and children during meals in fast food restaurants. *Pediatrics*, 133, e843–e849.

Renninger, K. A., & Hidi, S. (2016). *The Power of Interest for Motivation and Engagement.* New York: Routledge.

Riopel, M., Nenciovici, L., Potvin, P., Chastenay, P., Charland, P., Blanchette Sarrasin, J., & Masson, S. (2020). Impact of serious games on science learning achievement compared with more conventional instruction: An overview and a meta-analysis. *Studies in Science Education, 56,* 169–214.

Rosenberg, D., Depp, C. A., Vahia, I. V., Reichstadt, J., Palmer, B. W., Kerr, J., Norman, G., Jeste, D. V. (2010). Exergames for subsyndromal depression in older adults: A pilot study of a novel intervention. *The American Journal of Geriatric Psychiatry, 18,* 221–226.

Rutherford, T., Kibrick, M., Burchinal, M., Richland, L., Conley, A., Osborne, K., et al. (2010). Spatial temporal mathematics at scale: An innovative and fully developed paradigm to boost math achievement among all learners. Paper presented at AERA, Denver, CO.

Ryan, R. M., & Deci, E. L. (2000). Self-determination theory and the facilitation of intrinsic motivation, social development, and well-being. *American Psychologist, 55,* 68–78.

Ryan, R. M., Rigby, C. S., & Przybylski, A. (2006). The motivational pull of video games: A self-determination theory approach. *Motivation and Emotion, 30,* 347–363.

Sala, G., & Gobet, F. (2017). Does far transfer exist? Negative evidence from chess, music and working memory training. *Current Directions in Psychological Science, 26,* 515–520.

Sala, G., Tatlidil, K. S., & Gobet, F. (2018). Video game training does not enhance cognitive ability: A comprehensive meta-analytic investigation. *Psychological Bulletin, 144,* 111–139.

Saleem, M., & Anderson, C. A. (2013). Arabs as terrorists: Effects of stereotypes within violent contexts on attitudes, perceptions and affect. *Psychology of Violence, 3,* 84–99.

Saleem, M., Prot, S., Anderson, C. A., & Lemieux, A. F. (2017). Exposure to Muslims in media and support for public policies harming Muslims. *Communication Research, 44,* 841–869.

Schoneveld, E. A., Lichtwarck-Aschoff, A., & Granic, I. (2018). Preventing childhood anxiety disorders: Is an applied game as effective as a cognitive behavioral therapy-based program? *Prevention Science, 19,* 220–232.

Schüll, N. D. (2012). *Addiction by Design: Machine Gambling in Las Vegas.* Princeton: Princeton University Press.

Sestir, M. A., & Bartholow, B. D. (2010). Violent and nonviolent video games produce opposing effects on aggressive and prosocial outcomes. *Journal of Experimental Social Psychology*, 46, 934–942.

Sicart, M. (2009). *The Ethics of Computer Games*. Cambridge: The Massachusetts Institute of Technology Press.

Swing, E. L., Gentile, D. A., Anderson, C. A., & Walsh, D. A. (2010). Television and video game exposure and the development of attention problems. *Pediatrics*, 126, 214–221.

Tedeschi, J. T., & Quigley, B. M. (1996). Limitations of laboratory paradigms for studying aggression. *Aggression and Violent Behavior*, 1, 163–177.

Ventura, M., Shute, V., & Zhao, W. (2013). The relationship between video game use and a performance-based measure of persistence. *Computers & Education*, 60, 52–58.

Vygotsky, L. (1978). *Mind in Society: The Development of Higher Psychological Functions*. Cambridge: Harvard University Press.

Weaver, E., Gradisar, M., Dohnt, H., Lovato, N., & Douglas, P. (2010). The effect of presleep video-game playing on adolescent sleep. *Journal of Clinical Sleep Medicine*, 6, 184–189.

Weinstein, N., Przybylski, A. K., & Murayama, K. (2017). A prospective study of the motivational and health dynamics of Internet Gaming Disorder. *PeerJ*, 5, e3838.

Weis, R., & Cerankosky, B. C. (2010). Effects of video-game ownership on young boys' academic and behavioral functioning: A randomized, controlled study. *Psychological Science*, 21, 463–470.

Whiting, S. W., Hoff, R. A., & Potenza, M. N. (2018). Gambling disorder. In H. Pickard & S. H. Ahmed (Eds.), *The Routledge Handbook of Philosophy and Science of Addiction* (pp. 173–181). New York: Routledge.

Printed in the United States
by Baker & Taylor Publisher Services